SNOWED

SNOWED

Michigan's Worst Serial Killer Case

Ellen Wilson

Snowed
Michigan's Worst Serial Killer Case

All Rights Reserved © 2025 by Ellen Wilson

ISBN: 978-0-9897083-5-7

Cover Design by Carolyn Wilson

*Dedicated to the children,
past, present, and future.*

Contents

Preface..9

Chapter 1   4 Kids Killed...11

Chapter 2   A Break in the Case..................................14

Chapter 3   Christopher Busch, Happy-Go-Lucky Kid Killer..19

Chapter 4   Francis Shelden, Island Owner and Boy Procurer..29

Chapter 5   The Deadly Dream of Jill Robinson............52

Chapter 6   Officer Flynn's Two Gun Suicide................58

Chapter 7   Helen and Hastings....................................64

Chapter 8   Doug Wilson Knows the Car......................83

Chapter 9   Man About Town, Arch Sloan....................90

Chapter 10   The Magical Mystery Tour........................112

Chapter 11   The Mysterious John McKinney...............121

Chapter 12   Business as Usual, the 70s and Serial Killers...186

Chapter 13   The OCCK as Occult Ritual 203

Chapter 14   A Web of Connections..............................217

Illustrations ….…………………...………………………....227

Bibliography…………………………………………….....233

Preface

During the 1970s there were a series of seemingly unconnected murders throughout the United States. The murderers included Henri Lee Lucas, active in 1975-83, The Hillside Strangler, active 1977-78, David Berkowitz, of the Son of Sam case, apprehended in 1977, and the Atlanta Child Murderer, active in 1979-81. America was in the midst of what the FBI termed "serial killers" and more often than not, the term was applied to a lone assassin.

  Then there was the Oakland County Child Killer. A moniker invented by the press to describe the murders of four children near Detroit, Michigan during the years of 1976-77. The murders took place during the winter months and the killer was also called "the babysitter," another moniker invented by the press to describe the way the children were well taken cared for during their captivity and then subsequently arranged carefully at their drop off points. The image of this phraseology only served to imprint the idea inside the public mind that somehow the killer had a kindly, yet murderous intention towards these children.

  Although the hunt for the killer of these kids was one of the biggest in US history, and many dollars were invested in a long term investigation task force regarding the case, the investigation turned up very little in substantial leads for suspects, and, quite abruptly, the task force was disbanded and the case was basically shelved and only taken out and dusted off by a few well intentioned journalists writing about it on the anniversary of highlights of the case.

  While the case gained national attention for a brief period of time, it quickly fell off the radar and rarely would mention of it appear in books regarding serial killers such as David Berkowitz, who gave tantalizing tidbits of who or what, was behind the Son of

Sam murders and implored researchers to leave well enough alone, or John Wayne Gacy, with his murderous clown portraits and decrepit, stinking house full of buried bodies, described how John Norman was a participant in his serial killer cult. It's almost as if something or someone wanted the case to disappear. A case full of false leads, lies, and misdirection perpetually served up to the public by various officials in charge of the investigation, leading many to wonder why.

Chapter 1

4 Kids Killed

It was 1976, America's Bicentennial. The birth of the American nation on the 4th of July would be celebrated with great fanfare and decorum. In Michigan, this was also the year that four kids were killed by a serial killer—at least that was how the media and the police characterized it. There may have been others that were part of this chain of events, but in the Detroit area, this is what stuck in everyone's mind, and what came with it was a psychological trauma that infested the Southeast side of the state, and that kept continually creeping ominously through families and neighborhoods. Like a dark cloud hanging over the collective soul.

The first boy murdered was Mark Stebbins. He was twelve years old and lived in Ferndale, Michigan. Mark was last seen in Ferndale on February 15, 1976, leaving the American Legion Hall. He was there with his mother watching a pool tournament and he became bored and wanted to go home and watch a show on TV. Four days later his body was found in Southfield, Michigan in a parking lot of a strip mall. He had sustained lacerations on his wrists, ankles and neck indicating he had been bound for a lengthy period of time. Mark also had two distinctive lacerations on the back left side of his scalp investigators termed a "deer hoof pattern."[1] According to the original autopsy report the sustained marks to his wrists and ankles and were described as "artefacts" [2] or in layman's terms: Any change caused in the body after death that is likely to lead to misinterpretation of medically significant antemortem findings.[3] Also according to the official report generated by the Oakland County Coroner the apparent "ligature" mark of neck is considered an artifact and probably due to a jacket.[4]

The second victim was twelve-year-old Jill Robinson. Jill was abducted shortly before Christmas, on December 22, 1976. She had an argument with her mother and left the house on her bike with a backpack. Jill had told her mother many times that she had dreams of being shot in the head and killed. Her body was found the day after Christmas, December 26; it was determined the cause of death was a 12-gauge shotgun blast to the head.

Kristine Michelich, the third victim, was held the longest in captivity. She disappeared on January 2, 1977. She was found nineteen days later on January 21, 1977. She was found on Bruce Lane in Franklin Village, a wealthy semi-rural area.[5] According to

---

[1] Southfield Police Dept. "Narrative Report, Detective Bureau Follow-Up, 2003," 1.,
https://catherinebroad.blog/wp-content/uploads/2022/03/Binder-Final-1.pdf.

[2] Oakland County Medical Examiner. "Mark Douglas Stebbins Autopsy, 1976," 3.,
https://catherinebroad.blog/wp-content/uploads/2022/02/Stebbins-Autopsy-Final.pdf.

[3] Ambrish Kaushal, "Post Mortem Artefacts," Journal of Evolution of Medical and Dental Sciences. 8, no. 38 (2019): 1.

[4] Oakland County Medical Examiner, 3.

[5] M.F. Cribari, *Portraits in the Snow: The Oakland County Child Killings...Scandals and Small Conspiracies*, (Denver: Outskirts Press Inc., 2011), 7, 8.

celebrity psychiatrist Bruce Danto, she was placed there because he had sent the killer a message in the news.[6]

The fourth and final victim was Timothy King. Tim's sister had given him some change to buy some candy at the local store, and he left on his skateboard. His body was found, with his skateboard nearby, off of Gill Rd. Prior to the murder, Tim's mother was interviewed in a local newspaper and made a plea to the killer to treat him well and that when he came home she would make him his favorite fried chicken dinner. His autopsy showed that he was fed chicken before he was murdered.[7]

All children had been washed, cleaned and re-dressed in the clothes they had been wearing.[8]

If one looks at the other serial killings that were going on in roughly the same time period, one can discover a commonality between the killings and killers, the players, the scenarios, and what the general narrative was, etc. Quite possibly, a modus operandi can be derived by studying the evidence.

---

6 Tommy McIntyre, *Wolf in Sheep's Clothing: The Search for a Child Killer* (Detroit: Wayne State University Press, 1988), 115.
7 Cribari, *Portraits in the Snow*, 9, 10.
8 Dr Jerry Tobias, "Operation Burial Ritual", 1977, 3. https://catherinebroad.blog/wp-content/uploads/2021/02/OCCK-Files-1.pdf

Chapter 2

A Break in the Case

In 2005 the King family received news that the task force had reinvigorated the Oakland County Child Killer Case (OCCK). They were told there were new leads and that technological advances in criminal science could help solve the case. The family was very happy to hear of this development.[9]

Catherine King Broad, sister of Timothy King, victim, diligently began to read true crime websites about the OCCK case and noticed something. She noticed that although the case was reopened and the task force was rejuvenated, people who have information about the crime have gone to the police and get blown off time and time again. Broad began to realize huge mistakes might have been made in the case. She then visited her parent's house and read the box of news clippings her mother had collected over the years regarding the case looking for clues as to what went wrong. She decided to contact a friend who was a polygrapher and private investigator to review the case and determine what went wrong in the case if anything.

---

[9] "Chapter Title: 3. February 1976 to July 2006," *Decades of Deceit: A True Story of the King Family Search for the Oakland County Child Killer,* Unedited Comments, Dated April, May and July 2013 (Prod. by RW Productions, LLC. https://rwpmi.com. Distributed by Tim King Fund, 2013; Birmingham, MI), DVD.

What then happened was a series of coincidences that blew the case wide open and the Kings then had no doubt as to what was *really* happening regarding the case.

After Catherine King Broad had contacted her polygrapher/investigator friend he then told her he knew her other polygrapher friend, Patrick Coffey, who had practiced out of California. In fact, he said, he was going to a polygraphy conference and he was sure to be there. He said he would speak to Coffey about the both of them having a mutual friendship with her.

After the conference Coffey then called Broad and relayed some very exciting, yet disturbing information. Coffey told her a story. He said that at the end of his talk a man approached him and asked if he would speak to his polygrapher group in Southfield, Michigan regarding some of the issues he had just spoken of. Patrick Coffey told the man, Larry Wasser, that he had spent some of his teen years in that area. He went on to tell Wasser that one of the main reasons that he had chosen the polygraphy field was because his neighbor friend, Tim King, was murdered, and was a victim of the OCCK. He said he was so moved as to the hideousness of that crime he wanted to do something positive for humanity. Then, Wasser's demeanor totally changed. He told Coffey that he had performed an attorney privilege polygraph test for the man who was the murderer of Tim King. Immediately after divulging this information Wasser must have realized the grave consequences of what he had said. He said the perpetrator was now dead as well as the attorney who represented him, and that's why he had told him that. Because legally, Larry Wasser should not have revealed this information to anyone. He had breached attorney client privilege by telling Patrick Coffey this information. Even if the attorney and perpetrator were dead.

Dumbfounded, Catherine Broad deliberated what she would now do with this new information. Barry King, her father, told her that the MSP had broken off their relationship with Detective Cory Williams, from Livonia Police Department. Broad then decided to divulge this new information to Detective Williams. She called Detective Williams and told him the story about Patrick Coffey and Larry Wasser and added the caveat that she did not want him discussing this information with the MSP, because she felt they would either bury the information or obstruct the information. Williams agreed. He would not divulge this information to the MSP.

Detective Williams contacted Rob Moran, Assistant Prosecutor for Wayne County. Williams and Moran then developed a game plan regarding the new information that Catherine Broad had supplied. When questioned by Detective Williams, Larry Wasser was very evasive and told half truths about what he had said to Patrick Coffey. He said he couldn't remember and that the whole thing was pointless. They finally they wound up in court over an investigative subpoena with Assistant Prosecutor Moran saying to Wasser was that all they wanted was the name of the guy that he had polygraphed. Wasser refused.

The Supreme Court of Michigan then ruled that Larry Wasser had to give up the name of the individual he had polygraphed and divulged to Patrick Coffey. Wasser then says he thinks he remembers, so as not to perjure himself and never give up the name of the person polygraphed, he points to a folder regarding all the information investigators need to pursue the case. Legally if he had just given the name under the investigative subpoena and given the information to Detective Williams, no one would have ever learned who he was or how he acted regarding case information.

The person who Larry Wasser polygraphed that long ago day was named Christopher Busch. He was a suspect in the Oakland County Child Killer Case, and had been charged with various degrees of criminal sexual conduct against minors. Ironically, the day Catherine Broad called Detective Williams with the information she had received from Patrick Coffey was Busch's birthday. Busch had been dead for many years.[10]

The King family then learned about a legal group that was instrumental in protecting its self-interests regarding the information surrounding Christopher Busch. They first learned of the group when Larry Wasser went to testify under the investigative subpoena. This group consisted of Jane Burgess, attorney, Mr Feinberg, attorney, and Mr Wasser, polygrapher. Later on, they would find that then Oakland County Prosecutor, Jessica Cooper, would be instrumental in protecting this group. They discovered that Larry Wasser and Prosecutor Jessica Cooper were long time acquaintances, perhaps as long as four decades.

When Larry Wasser went to court to give testimony regarding the name he didn't want to divulge (Chrisopher Busch), it was Mr Feinberg who represented him. It was the attorney, Jane Burgess, who took Busch to see Wasser to be polygraphed in the first place. Apparently defense attorneys can take a client to a polygrapher in pedophile cases so that a judge would agree to a lesser charge or reduced jail time. Wasser also didn't complete an entire polygraph on Busch, because he learned that Mr Cabot from the MSP had already administered a polygraph and Busch had been cleared, indicating he had passed the polygraph test.

---

10 "Chapter Title: 4. July 2006 to January 2008 (Coffey/Wasser Story)," *Decades of Deceit: A True Story of the King Family Search for the Oakland County Child Killer.*

Because Jane Burgess, Busch's attorney, was dead, investigators talked to her husband, Larry Burgess. Mr Burgess referred to Mr Feinberg, Larry Wasser's attorney, as his partner. Mr Burgess said that the Busch family, who were quite wealthy, flew his wife, Jane, to Midland, Michigan and Atlanta, Michigan for his hearings regarding criminal sexual conduct against minors. They had even vacationed with the Busch family at the Busch's cottage at Ess Lake, in Northern Michigan.

Detectives Williams and Gray asked Larry Burgess if he though Christopher Busch could have been involved in the Oakland County Child Killings. Burgess acknowledged that he thought he could have been.[11]

---

11 "Chapter Title: 22. The Triangle," *Decades of Deceit: A True Story of the King Family Search for the Oakland County Child Killer.*

Chapter 3

Christopher Busch, Happy-Go-Lucky Kid Killer

A dossier on Christopher Busch would read like a who's who in the annals of pedophile suspects of the Oakland County Child Killer. A look at this suspect unearths the players surrounding the case and of at least one of the most likely networks that was active in procuring children. Busch was a pivotal piece in the network of pedophile activity, and that is why authorities wanted his role covered up at that point in time.

Christopher Busch was the son of a wealthy General Motors executive, Harold Lee Busch, who worked in the field of international finance. The family had a house in Bloomfield Township, an extremely wealthy area in the suburbs of Detroit, Michigan. They also had a house in Hillman, located in the northern lower peninsula of Michigan, a place where Christopher Busch would take young boys to sexually abuse them.[12]

In 1977 on the way to get his polygraph in the Circuit Court in Flint from his restaurant, The Scotsman, in Alma, Michigan, a business his father had bought for him, Busch divulged some pertinent information to the transporting officers. He told them that

---

12 Catherine Broad, "Special Assignment Timothy King Homicide, March 30, 1977," 62.,
https://catherinebroad.blog/wp-content/uploads/2022/02/Tullok-File-DPD-Info-documents-Final-1.pdf

he was a pedophile, he knew he had a problem, and it had started when he went to boarding school in England.[13] Prior to this confession by Busch, arresting officers had confiscated numerous items relating to his sexual habits and exploits: A spiral notebook containing sex pictures, seven 8 mm films, and one 8 mm film titled *The Collection*, along with other numerous magazines, comics, paraphernalia and airline tickets and receipts.[14] The same day, January 28, 1977, the confiscated items were checked into the Flint Violent Crimes unit they were handed over to the FBI. Then on April 26, 1978, the confiscated property was destroyed. This included the suitcase full of child pornography, the films and scrapbooks, and another suitcase which contained ropes. The destruction notification is clearly and boldly stamped on the property receipt.[15] Officers also confiscated two shotguns.[16]

Christopher Busch had a criminal accomplice named Gregory Greene who was polygraphed at the same time as Busch concerning the abduction of Mark Stebbins. They both independently told Cabot that they both arrived back in Michigan on February 14, 1976. This was the day prior to Mark Stebbins being abducted. Busch told Cabot he had arrived back in Detroit from a trip to England, and Greene said that he had been released from a psychiatric hospital five years earlier, and somehow met up with Busch. But they didn't remember all the details of what they did or where they went after arriving back in Michigan, but they

---

13 "Chapter Title: 7. Christopher Busch," *Decades of Deceit: A True Story of the King Family Search for the Oakland County Child Killer.*
14 *Decades of Deceit*, 7. Christopher Busch.
15 Flint City Violent Crime Tax Force, Fax Transmission, Property Receipt, (Flint, Michigan, October 2, 2012).
16 Flint City Violent Crime Tax Force, Fax Transmission.

arrived back at exactly the same date and told Cabot they were associates. Allegedly, no one was able to ascertain of how they knew or met each other.[17]

Busch told Cabot that he wanted to tie up a boy and abuse him. Greene told Cabot that Busch had in fact murdered Mark Stebbins.[18]

Retired detective Tom Waldron of the Flint Police Department vividly remembered the case involving Busch and Greene and couldn't believe that they passed their polygraphs with the MSP. He stated that he and the other officers thought for sure that they were the guys involved in the child killings. Waldron remembered the confiscated suitcases filled with child pornography and recalled that the FBI came to pick up the suitcase filled with pornography to analyze the victims who were involved.[19]

Waldron also said that Greg Greene told him where he had hid a pack of Polaroid pictures in his backyard. He had wrapped these pornographic pictures of kids in tin-foil and hid them in the snow under a downspout in his rear yard. Waldron went to Greene's house and located the pictures. As far as he could remember, Waldron said the pictures were not compared to the confiscated suitcase pornography pictures because Busch and Greene cleared

---

17 Catherine Broad, "Second of the three pages I am posting re: arrest of Busch and Green in Flint in the weeks before my brother's abduction", 106, *What the Hell is the Deal with the Oakland County Child Killer Investigation?* https://catherinebroad.wordpress.com/2013/03/10/second-of-three-pages-i-am-posting-re-arrest-of-busch-and-green-in-flint-in-the-weeks-before-my-brothers-abduction.
18 Livonia Police Department Narrative Report, D/Sgt. Cory Williams, OCCK Investigation, Incident # 77-00006883, July 31, 2007.
19 *Decades of Deceit*, 7. Christopher Busch.

the polygraph with Ralph Cabot of the MSP. He thought the pictures had been maintained as evidence at the Flint Police Department.[20]

It was in January of 1977 that Flint police arrested Greg Greene for criminal sexual conduct (CSC) 1st degree. Greene also told the arresting officers that Busch had murdered Mark Stebbins in February of 1976. He told police that Busch had a cabin up north where he would take boys and abuse them. He said he would assist officers any way he could and he had a map of how to get to the cabin in his van. Police searched the van and didn't find the map but found instead found two Polaroid pictures of a young boy involved in the CSC case and two pairs of young girl's panties.[21]

When the OCCK case was re-invigorated a search warrant was issued for obtaining evidence from the Busch residence. On October 28, 2008 there was a search warrant issued for trace evidence from the vent system. After fifty-six days the search warrant would become public unless there was a file extension or renewal request within the court system.

Barry King first saw reference to this search warrant regarding the Busch residence in 2011 when the attorney general presented it to Judge O'Brien during King's Freedom of Information Act (FOIA) request against the MSP. The judge had said, *"The search warrant had been suppressed and no one was*

---

20 Catherine Broad,"While police on the street are breaking their backs, a few levels up the chain-of-command, no one wants to connect the dots,"*What the Hell is the Deal with the Oakland County Child Killer Investigation?* https://catherinebroad.wordpress.com/2013/03/11/while-police-on-the-street-are-breaking-their-backs-a-few-levels-up-the-chain-of-command-no-one-wants-to-connect-the-dots.
21 Broad, "While police on the street are breaking their backs."

allowed to look at it including prosecutors and law enforcement officials."[22]

Barry King was very intrigued with this ruling and went down to obtain the file. The chief clerk wouldn't let him look at it.

Back in July of 2002 Barry King had filed a motion to intervene in the case. Assistant Oakland County Prosecutor Paul Walton, on behalf of Oakland County Prosecutor, Jessica Cooper, opposed Barry King's motion to intervene in the case. As King waited for Judge Small in 48th District Court to make a decision, Walton said that Judge Potts had already ruled that King couldn't look at the search warrant in regards to King's FOIA request, and Judge Small should rule in his (Walton's) favor. And without a hearing Judge Small issued an order that King couldn't intervene in the case.

King then filed a motion in 48th District Court for reconsideration of the order by pointing out some mistakes that Judge Small had made. And in April 2012 King filed a second FOIA to get the Oakland County Prosecutor Jessica Cooper's files on the search warrant case.

The Assistant Oakland County Prosecutor Paul Walton went before Judge Potts and said, "This is the wrong court judge, if you want to challenge the court order you have to go back to the other court. " King noted that effectively Walton and Cooper were telling Judge Potts that the case should be tried in the 48th District Court, but at the same time they were telling Judge Small in the 48th District Court that Judge Potts had already ruled on the case and that she should be the controlling decision.

---

22 Ibid.

King described the situation as a direct violation of judicial rules, where essentially you can't go into one court and say the light was red and go into another court and say the light was green. The exact same position must be taken in both courts. King has consistently argued that the court that issued the original order should be the deciding court that decides on the validity of the correctness of the decision.

King wrote a letter to Judge Small in March requesting a rule on the motion that he had filed that year. Shortly after he had sent the letter, he received a call from Gary Kline, the research attorney for Judge Small. Kline wanted to meet with King and shortly after that, on April 1st they met and Kline gave King the search warrant file. The file stated that Oakland County Prosecutor Jessica Cooper had stopped filing search warrant renewal orders in June of 2012. The affidavit also showed that Busch was very likely involved in the murder of children.[23]

More evidence concerning Christopher Busch as a suspect was divulged after an episode concerning the OCCK case aired on the *Investigative Discovery* Program. Narrator Matthew Phelps viewed the suicide photos of Busch and said they were very irregular, stating that he had never seen suicide photos that were partially blacked out before. These were the photos that the King's were given from the MSP. Phelp's statement prompted Erica McEvoy, sister of victim Kristine Mihelich, to obtain copies of the photos that were not blacked out.

---

23 "Chapter Title: 20. Search Warrant Report," *Decades of Deceit: A True Story of the King Family Search for the Oakland County Child Killer.*

Four adults called Barry King after viewing the show about the OCCK on the Investigative Discovery Program. Three of them were women.

One woman who saw the program told King that on March 21, 1977 she was driving down M59 north of Birmingham, Michigan. She said she Tim King in a car, which she described as a Gremlin. Tim had looked at her and did not seem at all bothered or nervous and appeared calm. She recognized him immediately because she had seen his picture in the paper. When she watched the *Investigative Discovery* program and saw Christopher Busch's photo she recognized him as driving the car that Tim was in. When she got to where she was going she immediately called the MSP and told them about the sighting. No one followed up on her call. And this was the biggest serial murder case in the country at the time. As far as Barry King could surmise this was the first time that that any of the suspects was seen with any one of the victims.

King turned this information over to investigating officers and they didn't seem overly thrilled with this information. The woman was very upset that no one wanted to listen to her story about seeing Tim King in a car with Christopher Busch. It was also an embarrassment to her because her son was a MSP cadet and he had talked to his superiors about the case which they told him they were investigating. One day he had went to work and a bunch of higher-ups were at the state police office and called him in and they told him they wanted his mom to be quiet. Regardless of this threat, his mother continued to try to get publicity for what she had seen and she had wanted to report. And Barry King said *God Bless her.*[24]

---

24 "Chapter Title: 21. Investigative Discovery Program," *Decades of Deceit: A True Story of the King Family Search for the Oakland County Child Killer.*

A man named Mel Paunovich contacted Barry King and asked if he could help with the case in any way. Paunovich was an investigator and evidence handler. King agreed to meet him and arranged a meeting with him at a local restaurant. Barry King's son Christopher, also went to the meeting and took notes.

Paunovich brought along several newspaper articles proving his expertise as an investigator and evidence handler. One of the articles cited described the first use of DNA evidence by prosecution in a murder case in Michigan.

Paunovich said he had worked on the Mark Stebbins case. He recounted how he was present at the crime scene and processed the evidence at the drop off site. He said the medical examiner was a drunk who did shoddy work and often failed to do tasks altogether. Paunovich said that he didn't think that the medical examiner would correctly process the information, so he contacted L. Brooks Patterson and Dick Thompson, and got their permission to remove the body from the scene and take it to the police department and check for trace evidence. When people criticized him about taking over the examination from the medical examiner at the time, he pointed out that L. Brooks Patterson had said it was the right thing to do and gave him permission.

He was very proud to have taken over the examination and to do the work himself as he believed that the evidence would have been lost otherwise. Paunovich told the Kings that he had pulled the hairs from the clothing himself. He said he gave the hairs to a female lab technician who thought they were animal hairs. They were actually human hairs. He said that there were hairs on the clothing that were animal hairs, but he was convinced some hairs were human.

He tossed the photos of the victim Mark Stebbins on the restaurant table. These were two back-to-back photos in a clear vinyl jacket. One was Stebbins's face at the crime scene with his eyes closed and the hood of his jacket up over his head. The other photo showed a shirtless body from the waist up as it lay on some type of examining table.

Paunovich described the body as he had encountered it at the crime scene. Mark Stebbins lay near a brick wall and was laid on his back with his hands folded on his chest or stomach. There were also ligature marks on his wrists and neck and a wound on his scalp.

Paunovich divulged his theories on who he thought killed Mark Stebbins. He thought the murderer was a member of law enforcement or someone extremely close to law enforcement because, "He seemed to know exactly what we were doing and where we were looking."

Based on theories that the killer always returned to the scene of the crime, he had some conversations with forensic psychiatrist Bruce Danto, and they decided to dress up a dummy which resembled the victim and place it where the body was dropped off. The police surveilled the scene for several days but detected no suspicious activity. The day they stopped their surveillance a funeral card from Mark Stebbins's funeral was placed right where the body and the dummy look-alike had been. Paunovich was convinced that it was the killer who had left the funeral card. He wondered if the card was still being held in crime scene evidence and if it could be checked again for prints or trace evidence using the latest technology.

Paunovich then went on to talk about several other cases he had worked on, detailing how he had been involved in busting a former Detroit Police Chief for stealing money from drug busts. He said that sources had told the police that the police chief had purchased cars and homes for cash. Paunovich said it was his idea to use the IRS to investigate, and they nailed the police chief. Paunovich also said they had enough evidence to indict Mayor Coleman Young on the same type of case and said everything was approved to go forward on this case but was shut down at a higher level by the feds, who said the word came down form President Carter that he did not want a popular black mayor indicted in an election year.

Chris King asked him if he was suspicious of Bruce Danto, criminal psychiatrist and law enforcement professional. Paunovich said he was, but seemed to think that Danto had an ironclad alibi for at least some of the murders.

Paunovich said the entire law enforcement system was rife with corruption. When asked if cops ever planted DNA he replied, "All the time."[25]

---

25 Chris King, Notes on Discussion with Mel Paunovich, Catherine Broad, *What the Hell is the Deal with the Oakland County Child Killer Investigation?* https://catherinebroad.blog/2019/03/06/notes-from-a-few-years-ago/.

Chapter 4

Francis Shelden, Island Owner and Boy Procurer

Detroit area business man Francis Shelden was many things. He was a millionaire, pilot, geologist, amateur botanist, university professor, land developer, oil consultant and market investor. He decided to buy an island on Lake Michigan.

At the end of the 1950s an obscure island in Lake Michigan named North Fox had one owner, Alma Plank. Then in 1959 Francis Shelden and his brother Alger, bought the island from Alma Plank. The Sheldens also owned a piece of property on the mainland in Leelanau County in Solon Township.[26]

"I was a pilot and plane owner, and flying to-and-fro to the island I had often wondered about the ownership of the various other islands in Lake Michigan and Lake Huron — especially the American islands, since reaching them wouldn't involve border-crossing and all the hassles of customs and immigration I had to go through every time I touched down at Gore Bay on Manitoulin and then again returning to Detroit," Shelden said.[27]

The Shelden brothers announced their plans for a vacation destination for aircraft owners. Over the next few years, Omena

---

26 Katherine Craker Firestone, *The Fox Islands North and South: Lake Michigan Islands, Volume II*, (Northport: Michigan Islands Research., 1996), 177.
27 Firestone, *The Fox Islands*, 178.

contractor, Frank Kalchik, got a crew to clear and grade the landing area into a 3,300-foot-long by 250-foot-wide strip.[28]

Conservation Officer Gerald Battle remembered a strange encounter he had on North Fox Island. Battle kept a detailed journal of his conservation activities and the day of August 18, 1964 stood out for him. The day's entry read, "I accompanied pilot Van Weiren to North Fox Island, and made a game census for a game breeder's license application." But he neglected to add the strange encounter that took place that day in in the journal. Battle and Van Weiren came across an unidentified boy around nine to ten years old and a woman. Battle remembered that the boy looked very scared. He also had an intuition that the woman was not the boy's mother.

"There was something in her manner, and the manner of the kid, that there was quite a bit of tension there. But at the time I thought, *That's not what I'm here for. I'm here for a game breeder's license.*"

Soon after the strange encounter with the boy and the woman, Battle and Van Weiren were whisked away by Francis Shelden.

Battle reminisced about Northern Michigan and the area around the Fox Islands. "If you've been around Leelanau very long there's something about that Manitou Passage. The Indians believed there was something special out there, and I believe there is something special." he said.[29]

And then Francis Shelden got busted — on CSC charges involving minor boys. And a whole lot of other people got busted,

---
28 Ibid.
29 Alan Campbell, "Stories Spark Memories of Strange Encounters on North Fox Island," *Leelanau Enterprise*, April 3, 2014, Local News.

associates of his, and authorities began to discover a very large transatlantic network of boy procurers, abusers and filmmakers. Some of them did time, but not Shelden. He escaped.

The story was broke by intrepid journalist, Marilyn Wright, writing for the *Traverse City Record-Eagle*. It was good and concise reporting, and for those who actually know what investigative journalism is these days, how rare it is these days — read it for the gem it was. Apparently the silencers of the media had not gotten to Marilyn.

Marilyn started writing about the North Fox pedophile ring in 1977, detailing the man Francis Shelden and his deeply woven connections. She wrote how his enterprises hop-scotched across the county: Oil leases in Kansas, a ski lodge in Aspen, a land investment company in Denver, the Monroe Creek development in Charlevoix, and extensive stock holdings in a West Indies Trust company.

Police records stated that Shelden cleaned out his Ann Arbor and North Fox Island residences of incriminating evidence shortly after Gerald Richards, an associate of Shelden's in Brother Paul's Children's Mission, was arrested on CSC charges. This was in July 1976, approximately one week before state police obtained a search warrant for his Ann Arbor residence. A warrant was then issued for his arrest on December 7, 1976, and a second warrant was issued a week later.[30]

The FBI was very aware that Shelden and an associate in Michigan were, in their own words, "deeply involved in child

---

30 Marilyn Wright, "Shelden Left a Trail of Shock," *Traverse City Record Eagle*, December 14, 1977,
http://newspaperarchive.com/us/michigan/traverse-city-record-eagle/1977/12-14/.

pornography on a wide scale."[31] The FBI also reported that Shelden and an associate were involved in a foster care home in Washington, D.C.[32]

Francis Shelden's brother, Alger Shelden Jr., reportedly told authorities that he was hiring security personnel for North Fox Island, the site of the alleged pornography operation(s), to keep unauthorized police away. Who the "unauthorized police" were was not specified.

Francis Shelden had a house in Charlevoix and was well known to members of the small lakeside town. The community was further jolted when Shelden disappeared, and an eighteen-year-old youth whom he had befriended when the boy was nine committed suicide. Apparently he had wrote the boy from Miami when he was on the run explaining that he would be away for a while working on some personal problems, but didn't want the boy to think he had forgotten about his promise to send him to college.

Authorities believe that the supposed benevolent "benefactor" had ulterior motives when he took kids on hunting trips to his island, skiing trips to Aspen, or beach parties at his family estate in Antigua, or when he set up trust funds for college educations for particular youths.

On the same day that Shelden mailed a letter from Miami to the youth who committed suicide in Charelvoix, another letter was purportedly sent by him to Cranbrook Science Institute in Bloomfield Hills, Michigan. This letter submitted his resignation as a member of the board of directors to that exclusive educational facility. This letter was postmarked from Kearney, New Jersey,

---

31 Federal Bureau of Investigation, Airtel Communication from Denver to Detroit, *Frances Duffield Shelden — Fugitive,* November 10, 1977, 2.
32 FBI, Airtel Communication.

where Adam Starchild, another associate of Shelden's, was located. Shelden and Starchild were also involved in the Church of the New Revelation and the Ocean Living Institute, which were located in New Jersey.

FBI agents planned to to conduct a follow up interview with another youth who was a frequent traveling companion of Shelden. This young man was also attending college on a similar trust fund arrangement. Authorities said the young man had been driving Francis Shelden's car which had been abandoned at the Charlevoix airport. The airport staff verified that the car had been driven away but they couldn't say who drove it.

Around the same time frame in October of 1976 when Shelden was busy mailing letters, Starchild was reportedly negotiating the sale of Shelden's plane through Combsgate Aviation in Denver, Colorado.

Then in January of 1977, Shelden resigned from the board of directors of Boys Republic, Inc., a Farmington Hills residential center for the treatment of emotionally disturbed young boys. The envelope bore the name and address of the family firm, Shelden Land Co., and was postmarked January 19, 1977 from Detroit.

That was the last public word from Frances Shelden — his trail then went cold.[33]

The Detroit Division of the FBI said that on March 14, 1977, a detective from the MSP in Charlevoix stated that approximately a week to ten days earlier a twin Bonanza Airplane #715-U departed the Charlevoix Airport with a flight plan that included National, Tennessee. The FBI noted that through previous investigations both

---

33 Wright, "Trail of Shock."

Francis Shelden and another [redacted] individual had used the term Big Brothers in regards to their sexual activities. The FBI agent further noted that Shelden was involved in obtaining a boy's camp in Tennessee which had been recently indicted in a sexual abuse case.[34]

An investigator with the Tennessee Attorney General's Office, Pete Bouldin, confirmed what the FBI had noted about the sexual abuse case in that state. Bouldin said that the New Jersey Church of the New Revelation turned up in their investigation into Boys Farm, Inc. The farm claimed to be a rehabilitation center for juvenile offenders but authorities said it was actually a center for homosexual activities. "There's no church," Boudin said. "It's just a referral agency which distributes the pornography around the country."

When the Tennessee police raided Boys Farm they seized films and photographs depicting homosexual acts between kids at the farm. Police also confiscated lists of "sponsors" from throughout the United States. Escaped millionaire Francis Shelden was listed as one of the more than 270 sponsors.[35]

Police stated that the crimes were perpetrated on North Fox Island under the cover of Brother Paul's Children's Mission. Shelden was listed as a director of Brother Paul's. His associate Dyer Grossman, was listed as vice president, and Gerald Richards, another pedophile ring accomplice, who was listed as president and

---

34 United States Department of Justice, Federal Bureau of Investigation, Detroit, Francis Duffield Shelden, (Unlawful Flight to Avoid Criminal Prosecution — Sexual Criminal Conduct),14.
35 Marilyn Wright, "Unrest Helped Unravel Nationwide Web," *Traverse City Record Eagle*, April 4, 1977.

the director of the "nature camp," was serving a two-to-ten-year term in Jackson Prison for a CSC charge of a ten-year-old boy.[36]

In 1977 Gerald Richards participated as a witness before the Senate Subcommittee to Investigate Juvenile Delinquency. Senate members wanted to know how he got involved in the production of child pornography films. Richards told them. He explained that there were some ads in various magazines seeking that type of pornographic film material, and he had the access and could provide it for the people who wanted it. He then met a man who could assist in making places available to film the boy models.[37]

Richards stated that it was a business that moved back and forth across states and over international boundaries.[38] He said that one his sponsors was also going to open up a home, similar to Boy's Farm in Tennessee, in Washington, D.C.[39]

He then explained the grooming process. They would look for a boy that had a poor family background as far as a father image was concerned. Because there was no father figure, the boy would look for a man to be his friend. The photographer he explained, is like a father substitute many times. Second, he said, they very seldom have any kind of religious or moral background. And third, they meet the attributes that are required for the boy pornography business. It was part of the whole picture of grooming a model involved in their pornography business.[40]

---

36 Marilyn Wright, "Fugitive Warrants Requested," *Traverse City Record Eagle*, February 11, 1977.
37 Sexual Exploitation of Children, Hearings Before the Subcommittee on Crime of the Committee on the Judiciary House of Representatives, Statement of Gerald S. Richards, Jackson State Prison, Jackson, Mich., 34.
38 Sexual Exploitation of Children, Hearings Before the Subcommittee, 40.
39 Ibid., 41.
40 Ibid., 36.

He talked about various men in the grooming process that used techniques to desensitize the child. Richards stated that it was elaborated in the literature promoted by various pedophiles and was a coordinated effort.[41] He described it as a type of idea or philosophy among this type of pedophile, where they believed they were reliving, or emulating an old Dorian Greek philosophy of a man and boy relationship that encompassed mind, body and spirit. It was a metaphysical thing to them, he said.[42]

The writings of these men detailed their belief system and relayed their interwoven network that transcended national boundaries and was for them a spiritual quest. The vast network also revealed how powerful they were.

It was in 1993 that the District Attorney of Santa Barbara County California tried to prosecute Michael Jackson for molesting thirteen-year-old Jordan Chandler. The district attorney's office seized numerous erotic books for evidentiary purposes. One of the books found locked in a filing cabinet in Michael Jackson's bedroom was a compilation of boys engaged in various activities, and in about 90% of the pictures the boys were naked. The book is edited by Georges St. Martin and Ronald C. Nelson. Georges St. Martin was the pseudonym of Martin Swithinbank, who was a contributor to the NAMBLA (North American Man/Boy Love Association) Bulletin. He was deported to England after his prison sentence of sodomizing young boys on Long Island, New York. Ronald C. Nelson was the pseudonym of Ronald Drew, a New York teacher who was arrested and indicted for selling obscene

---

41 Ibid., 44.
42 Ibid., 38.

photographs depicting children involved in various forms of deviant sexual conduct and intercourse.[43]

Swithinbank spent more than forty years of his life in America, where he had obtained in 1951 a Fulbright Scholarship from Harvard's School of Business Administration. Analyzing his stay in the US, along with his devious dealings in the shadowy network of high-end pedophile rackets, reveals clues as to the depths of the transatlantic child abuse links and why Yale's Reverend George Parker Rossman (who operated under various aliases and helped set up Brother Paul's Children's Mission on North Fox Island with Francis Shelden) escaped justice.[44]

During the years of 1953-1972, George Parker Rossman was an American Yale Divinity School Professor. He was also a leading figure in an international abuse network and associate of boy lovers which included Dr Morris Fraser, Dennis W Nichols (aka D.W. Nichols) — a Sociology Professor at Western Michigan University (WMU), in Kalamazoo, Michigan, from the 1960s into the 1980s, (who would have heard of academic Jack Fritscher, lover of Robert Mapplethorpe, and who was on the board of directors of the Kalamazoo Institute of Arts), and Martin Swithinbank (British Harvard Fulbright scholar, photographer and who co-founded NAMBLA in 1977).

Martin Swithinbank was a professional photographer whose works appeared in *Encyclopedia Britannica* and *Life Magazine* as well as many other publications. He soon found his photography

---

43 @CASSANDRACOGNO, "1981: NAMBLA's distinguished British Pedigree, Martin Swithinbank, & the NY Director of Sexual Abuse Prevention," *Bits of Books, Mainly Biographies*.
44 Ellen Wilson, "OCCK is Huge," *Wilson's Words and Pictures*, https://wilsonswordsandpictures.com/occk-is-huge/.

skills came in handy distributing boy sex abuse images. Swithinbank was also connected to the 1973 Long Island Fraser/Rossman international boy sex ring.[45]

In a 1977 interview, D.W. Nichols told Daniel Tsang of the *Midwest Gay Academic Journal* (a journal which was published through University of Michigan, Ann Arbor, Michigan, and was the same school that Martin's cousin glacierologist Charles Swithinbank did his research, and where Francis Shelden obtained a degree in the related field of geology) that he worked with Book Explorers Inc. This was the company that published Swithinbank's *The Boy: A Photographic Essay*, in 1964 and *Boys Will Be Boys!*, in 1966.[46]

D.W. Nichols also discussed George Parker Rossman in the Tsang interview. Rossman was arrested in 1973 with Dr Morris Fraser, Belfast child psychologist, and others in a Long Island, New York boy sex ring bust. Nichols mentioned that George Parker Rossman had received a mailing list from Nichols and Swithinbank's Book Explorers company. It is assumed by investigators that it is the same list discovered in Nichols and Swithinbank's Aquarious Press operation which was raided in 1970, the same year that Nichols left Book Explorers. Nichols also mentioned that George Parker Rossman published his book on boy sex trafficking, *Boys for Sale* through Book Explorers using the alias of Jonathon Drake. D.W. Nichols, Martin Swithinbank and George Parker Rossman were obviously all very good friends.[47]

---

45 @CASSANDRACOGNO, "1981: NAMBLA' distinguished British Pedigree," *Bits of Books, Mainly Biographies*.
46 Ibid.
47 Ibid.

In 1970, D.W. Nichols ended his association with Book Explorers, Inc., and on June 10, 1970, the Associated Press reported that, "$1 million worth of pornographic material," was raided in a Cape Cod film shop, Aquarius Press, located in Barnstable, Massachusetts. The raid contained hundreds of thousands of colored slides, photographs, and brochures. Three men were arrested in the bust: D.W. Nichols, Martin Swithinbank, and Norval Shutz. Authorities discovered a filing cabinet containing thousands of names and addresses from around the world.[48]

D.W.Nichols wrote an article, "The Existential Approach to the Causation and Maintenance of Male Homosexuality," for a publication called the *Mattachine Review*. An early homosexual advocacy group, The Mattachine Society was created by Harry Hay, and was connected to the Communist Party in the 1950s. Guy Straight, a sex abuse pornographer, was also connected to Harry Hay. Guy Straight "was one of the nation's leading pornographers... he had cornered the market on the production of 'kiddie porn'."[49]

On April 14, 1977, Newark FBI corresponded with an individual who did not know where Francis Shelden was but he knew that the Detroit Bank and Trust Company, Detroit Michigan, was questioning Shelden's signatures on trust documents in their possession. The bank wanted to obtain new signatures from Shelden.[50]

The District Attorney in Port Huron had managed to bury Shelden's arrest warrant in the bottom of their paperwork giving the

---

48   Ibid.
49   "Guy Straight," *NewgonWiki*, https://www.newgon.net/wiki/Guy_Strait.
50   Federal Bureau of Investigation, Airtel Communication from Newark to Detroit, *Frances Duffield Shelden — Fugitive*, November 10, 1977, 82.

fugitive more than enough time to get his affairs in order and flee the country to Amsterdam to become a naturalized Dutch citizen protected from extradition.

Adam Starchild was a pedophile offshore tax attorney who worked for Francis Shelden incorporating companies set up as fronts for child pornography and prostitution. In September of 1976 Shelden had given Starchild power of attorney to transfer all of his assets, including North Fox Island, into an offshore trust called the *Trust Company of the Virgin Islands, Ltd.* Then two years later in 1978 he appointed Edward Brongersma, a Dutch Senator known for his pedophile advocacy activities, as the primary trustee of his offshore estate using an attorney based in Amsterdam.[51]

Brongersma was part of pornography network and an alleged double agent of the KGB, according to investigator Marcel Vervloesm. This pornography network included Edward Brongersma, Frits Salomonson (a lawyer for Queen Beatrix of the Netherlands), and Joris Demmink, a Dutch Justice Department official. Also included in the network was Gerrit Ulrich, a German computer scientist who was also an alleged double KGB agent. Their supervisor was Wanja Gotz, a KGB liason officer posted in Dresden, Germany, at the same time as Vladimir Putin. Apparently their mission was to train teams of agents to power the kompromat (English equivalent: compromise) and blackmail celebrities and government officials.[52]

Frances Shelden was trying to maintain his trust fund monies after he had fled overseas and became embroiled in a lawsuit trying to do so. The events leading to the involvement of

---

51 "Eye of the Chickenhawk," *The Hotstar*,
https://thehotstar.net/eyeofthechickenhawk.html.
52 Wilson, "OCCK is Huge."

Francis Shelden with Adam Starchild and the creation of the revocable inter vivos trust, a legally binding situation where he would control his assets while he was still alive, was precipitated by a call from Dyer Grossman.

Francis Shelden received this call from Dyer Grossman in July of 1976, where he largely testified in code to the court discussing the situation. Grossman said that their associate, Gerald Richards, was having severe "difficulties" and Richards might involve Shelden in these "difficulties," and therefore might very well become the subject of blackmail by Richards. Shelden testified that Grossman "suggested that it might be wise for me to leave the country for a while...to await events." Francis Shelden's main concern was protecting his assets, especially his negotiable stocks. He asked Grossman for advice in this situation. Grossman said he should contact Adam Starchild, (alias of Malcolm Willis McConahy) who was an investment counselor specializing in offshore investments.[53] According to Francis Shelden, he had never personally met Adam Starchild, but telephoned him in New Jersey and asked him for financial advice. Starchild recommended that Shelden bring his stock certificates to New Jersey and he would discuss the matter further with him. Shelden then met with Starchild in New Jersey, trust certificates in hand.

Then a meeting took place between Francis Shelden, his brother Alger Jr., L. Bennet Young (his current attorney at the time), and Adam Starchild, at the Shelden's family house in Antigua, British West Indies. There was a general discussion as to how Francis Shelden's assets should be managed. Starchild took the

---

53 "Adam Starchild," Wikipedia.
https://en.wikipedia.org/wiki/Adam_Starchild.

position that a trust was essential in managing a financial relationship with Shelden, and recommended an irrevocable trust. L. Bennet Young expressed doubt that a trust was necessary, and took the position that in all events concerning Francis Shelden's financial situation an irrevocable trust would be especially unwise. At the insistence of Young, a revocable trust was finally decided upon. And on October 9, 1976, Francis Shelden, as settlor, appointed L. Bennet Young as protector, with the concurrent power to remove trustees and appoint successor trustees. Adam Starchild, as the director of The Trust Company of the Virgin Islands Ltd., acknowledged the appointment of Young as protector of the trust. Following the execution of the trust instrument, Francis Shelden returned to Europe.[54]

Safely ensconced in the Netherlands, Francis Shelden began writing pornographic literature in earnest. Shelden started the newsletter, *PAN: A Magazine about Boy-love*, under his pen name, Frank Torey. He also used this alias when he was in North American when he wrote for another newsletter called *Better Life Monthly*, or BLM, which savvy readers knew as "Boy Lovers Monthly."

The first volume of *PAN* was published by Spartacus International in 1979. Spartacus was a publishing house and a network owned by John Stamford, who had fled the United Kingdom for Amsterdam under similar circumstances as Francis Shelden. In 1972 he had been charged with operating a mail-order child pornography business.[55]

Stamford had started his adult life as a Catholic priest in Brighton, UK, then went on to develop what was thought by some

---

54 National Bank of Detroit v. Francis D. Shelden, 730 F.2d 421 (6th Cir. 1984).
55 "Eye of the Chickenhawk," *The Hotstar*.

to be the biggest gay business empire in the world. Billed as the world's most comprehensive homosexual information guide, it sold at least a quarter of a million copies per year in its heyday of the mid to late 1970s.[56]

The Spartacus network in actuality hid behind the *Spartacus* publication, which masqueraded as a holiday guide for gays on travels around the world. The information in the guide pointed out places that were attractive for pedophiles. Stamford did finally face charges, and was accused of using the guide and publication as a front for procuring children for prostitution.

Apart from the publishing of a guide that pandered to pedophiles in easy kid rape areas of the world, John Stamford faced other charges as an accomplice of hotel owners in these pedophile paradises in various countries like Thailand and the Philippines. What the hotel owner did was to act as an intermediary between Stamford and his pedophile clients. The clients would tell Stamford what sort of child they were looking for and in which country. Stamford then would get in touch with his local contacts who would provide the children according to order.

Two important lists were leaked to journalists regarding this network. The first one was called the Spartacus list, and was comprised of Belgian subscribers to Stamford's *Spartacus* publication. Investigators thought that many of these people were homosexuals looking for other adult homosexuals and were not involved in pedophilia. The second list was of worldwide clients

---

[56] "Part 2: The Whole Story of the Spartacus International Gay Guide, by its founder John D. Stamford and how Bruno Gmünder made the bargain of his life," *BrunoLeaks*.
https://brunoleaks.blogspot.com/2011/08/2teil-die-ganze-geschichte-vom.html.

who paid Stamford for his "Holiday Help Portfolios." This was the euphemism Stamford used for payments he received to provide children to pedophiles in hotels. Stamford's notes include credit card payments, along with descriptions of the age and type of children that were requested together with the services the children were to perform.

John Stamford conveniently died in prison while awaiting trial in Belgium. Investigators believed that it would have been an open and shut case if Stamford had not died.

This was a similar situation to when Christopher Busch died and the OCCK investigation task force was shut down, and thus the active investigation. When John Stamford died the investigation was halted and according to investigators, had gathered dust ever since. None of the information uncovered in the investigation was shared with other countries. Investigators felt that if they could persuade Belgian authorities to open up the case file located in Turnhout in the north of the country they would discover a great deal of interesting information about British pedophiles.

The Belgian networks operated under a cover organization called CRIES, (pronounced cree-es in English) which was a so-called center of research, Centre de Recherches et de l'Information sur l'Enfance et la Sexualite (Center for Research and Information into Childhood and Sexuality). This "Center for Research" was in fact a club for pedophiles from all over Europe. The problem was that CRIES which had been operating under the auspices and full approval of UNICEF, was fully dependent on UNICEF, and whose computer system allowed "clients" to discretely find young children. One of the four men who was eventually convicted in the pedophile scandal was the very head of UNICEF in Belgium.

The four defendants in the pedophile case in Belgium freely admitted to having sex with children and using the CRIES network to organize meetings with fellow pedophiles. At these meetings they freely exchanged photos of abused children and even named some of the children.

On a 1-10 scale of depravity, some wondered how bad the CRIES network was. One investigator who worked the case, Patrick De Baets said it was about a 9.0. De Baets had worked the Dutroux case, investigating the Xs (victims and informants) and said he had seen and heard things that totally defied the imagination. He had learned what normal people thought was impossible, does indeed exist and take place. De Baets spoke of unnameable acts with children, and even babies. These were people who met up and exchanged photos and information with others who were of like mind in their levels of depravity. He made clear which was confirmed by many sources that the contents of the CRIES files were apocalyptic in nature.[57]

The Dutroux affair was the case where Patrick De Baets investigated the X victims and informants in Belgium. Investigator Jean-Marc Connerrotte took over the serial killer case involving young girls and he landed Dutroux in prison and rescued two girls from the dungeon hell where Dutroux had kept them. Of course Connerrotte was very popular. But because he did such a good job the highest court in Belgium decided to remove him from the case.

---

57 C.R.I.E.S (Belgium), *kaztigrfiles*,
https://sites.google.com/site/kaztiggrfile/paedo-mags/cries/.

The same hour the decision was made, spontaneous protests started all over the country.[58]

The populace of that country was so disgusted that a huge march on the capitol was organized. "...the fire brigade in Liege drove their trucks downtown and turned their water cannons against the Justice building to demonstrated that "the whole judicial system needs a good cleanup." There were 300,000 people at the White March in Brussels, Belgium, protesting against judicial corruption regarding the Dutroux case.[59]

There was also a French connection to the OCCK case in regards to a novel that was written and translated to French. Some people speculated that this novel could have been written by Dr Bruce Danto, because whoever wrote it had an intimate familiarity with the case that only an insider could have had regarding personal relationships and psychological symbolism.

The Oakland County Child Killer "novel," was written under the alias, Michael L. Parrot.

There are characteristics of Dr Danto within the pages of the novel. For one, Dr Danto takes on the starring role, or hero, of the story, while the killer, of course, is the villain. So whoever wrote the book would have had to have been inside Danto's mind, because there is a definite literary fingerprint that is unique regarding his personal style and insider knowledge of the case.

The tone is set before the novel starts with a quote by the psychiatrist hero of the novel at the beginning of the book, Dr Elliot

---

58 Ellen Wilson, "OCCK and International Connections Part IV," *Wilson's Words and Pictures*, https://wilsonswordsandpictures.com/tag/edgar-bronfman/.
59 Wilson, "OCCK is Huge."

Denton. He is addressing the Oakland County Task Force, a special unit set up to investigate the serial killings. He says:

"This killer's quite a showman, too. He goes to great lengths in preparing his victims' bodies for display, washing them, washing their clothes, trimming their nails, even carefully laying the bodies in the snow as if he were going to be judged on the finished product. He has a morbid need for people to look at his work. He's a maniac. A real squirrel. Only he's a demented squirrel that gathers children instead of nuts."

With this quote hero Dr Denton lays out the killer for us in a neat package. In fact, he wants us to notice his expertise and his showmanship. Not unlike the killer he describes.

In an academic paper analyzing the Oakland County Child Killer Dr Danto basically says the same thing which is described in the novel:

"I would add to this discussion that the serial murderer usually has an obsessive-compulsive pattern to his killing, as well as his choice of victim. His homicidal behavior is repetitive and frequently tells a story of his conflicts. For example, in the Oakland County (Michigan) child killings, the murderer selected children in the same age range, sodomized the boys and forced the girls into oral sexual acts, was gentle in his method of killing, washed the bodies and dressed the victims, and always left the body where it was sure to be found. He acted out a story in which he replaced the natural parents of the child he abducted, committed a sexually perverse act on the child, then murdered him or her; in so doing, he showed the parents how poorly they protected their child and how great their loss could be. The parents are his victims. He kills children to avenge some childhood hurt induced by his own parents toward whom he is now venting angry feelings. He checks on the parental loss by attending the child's funeral or following it on television. We know this because he dropped a funeral visitor's card where the body of the first murdered child was found."[60]

There are characters within the story that seem to be composites of people involved in, or tangential to, this serial killing shock case. There is a gallery owner named Alexander who himself is a talented modernist sculptor, mirroring perhaps gallery owner John McKinney and Senator Jack Faxon, artist and collector.

This owner of the gallery, (called White Gallery) is interested in a series of photos taken by a Catholic priest named Francis Dole, perhaps resembling Francis Shelden (wealthy Michigan native involved in an international pedophile ring), who speaks with another priest, Father McKinnen, about the photos, again mirroring John McKinney gallery owner. Both of these people, McKinney and Shelden, could have had some type of "priest" position within the possible occultic (Dorian philosophy) circles they ran in. The photos taken by Christopher Busch confiscated by the FBI and alleged sketch of Mark Stebbins are alluded to here also.

The character of Lieutenant Davis has members of the task force learn everything they can about sacrifices in witch's covens. He also states he knows there is two witches' covens in the area, maybe more, and to check them out. He then sends them on a little trip to see Gondella the witch who was a fortune teller that had a vision of what the killer looked like.

Francis Dole talks to a mechanic named Harold Wilson, perhaps modeled after Doug Wilson, who knew the makes of cars

---

60 Bruce L. Danto, "A Psychiatric View of Those Who Kill," in *The Human Side of Homicide*, ed., Bruce L. Danto, John Bruhns, and Austin H. Kutscher, (New York: Columbia University Press, 1982), 13,14.

like the back of his hand being a car designer and was hypnotized by the FBI after he had divulged he had seen Tim King in the parking lot of the pharmacy before he was abducted.

In the true crime book, *Wolf in Sheep's Clothing,* Detective Robertson portrays Dr Danto as a media darling, where "…the media's all over him. They call him to see what he thinks about all this, and he responds. The the media comes to us and says 'Danto says this' or 'Danto says that,' and that puts us in a position where we either have to respond or stonewall."

The French version of the novel, *The Oakland County Child Killer,* is entitled *Pardonnez-moi vos* offenses, and is written by the same author as the English version.

The book is written as part of a serie noire (dark series) that was written as part of a collection of occult practices which are sequentially numbered. The magickal workings of interlocking occult groups who "play" or make "art" on various themes. It is an updated version of the "Theatre Memory System" of Robert Fludd, English Renaissance occultist.

Instead of the heroic self-congratulatory quote by the character Elliot Denton of the English version, we get this note from the book's editor/translator, Jane Fillion:

"This book was designed from real facts. During the 1977 summer, several children were murdered in the northern suburbs of Detroit. A Special Team of three hundred policemen worked night and day for six months to discover the killer. The series ended abruptly, and the assassin was never found."

The noir series was very popular in France, and created by Marcel Duhamel, a screenwriter and actor active in surrealist, avant-garde occult circles.[61]

There were those investigating the case that felt the most common geographic profiling error made concerning Francis Shelden was to refer to his pedophile procurement as exclusively operating within the confines of North Fox Island. It gave the impression that he was always operating in a remote section of North West Michigan, far away from the hub of Oakland and Wayne Counties.

The fact was that North Fox Island was merely his film set, which due to weather conditions, could only be used three to four months out of the year for pornographic boy films.

The actually belly of the beast was Shelden's condo in Ann Arbor, Michigan. It was the corporate headquarters location for the entirety of his enterprise, rightfully called "Child Pornography, Inc." His operations could more accurately be referred to as the "Ann Arbor Pornography" ring. His long term presence and post graduate work in Ann Arbor lead one investigator to believe that the University of Michigan was likely a hub of academic pedophilia. This was the location of his extensive child pornography client list, which some researchers felt contained the name(s) of the person or persons who paid him to organize and direct the abduction of Mark Stebbins.

Investigators who reviewed some of Shelden's "poetic" boy love writing, thought that it was clear that Shelden had scoped out

---

61 Wilson, "OCCK is Huge."

places where there were likely to be many of his "fellow traveler" pedophiles.[62]

---

[62] Catherine Broad, "Shelden's Stain on all of Michigan and Beyond," https://catherinebroad.blog/2022/02/03/sheldens-stain-on-all-of-michigan-and-beyond/

Chapter 5

The Deadly Dream of Jill Robinson

On December 22, 1976, 12-year-old Jill Robinson had an argument over household chores with her mother, Karol Robinson. At the height of the quarrel, Karol told Jill to leave until she could become part of the family. Jill then went to her bedroom, packed some clothes, and put them into her denim backpack, along with a blue and green plaid blanket.

She put on her bright orange winter jacket, and pulled on her boots, and donned her blue knit cap with the yellow design on the border. She then walked out the door.

Karol was divorced from Jill's father, and she had expected Jill to ride her bike over to his house. When she didn't return home after she had phoned him, he called the police at 11:30 pm and reported her missing.

She was never seen alive again.

Her body was found at 8:45 am the day after Christmas, December 26, 1976. Jill's body was dropped alongside Route I-75 just north of 16 Mile Rd., in Troy, Michigan. Her killer had laid her down on her back alongside the snowy shoulder of the road, then blew the top of her head off with a 12-gauge shotgun. She was wearing her denim backpack.

Despite the many reports that were telephoned to police of seeing a girl Jill's age in cars, or traveling along I-75, no valid leads were developed. There was no real information regarding her disappearance or whereabouts for four days, or who the murderer(s) might possibly be. It was easy for police to determine the kind of shotgun and shell used, it was a common variety easily obtainable in any number of local gun and hardware stores.

The case took a strange turn when Jill's bike was found by a neighborhood boy in the afternoon of the 27th of December behind the Valenti and Lieberman offices on N. Main St. in Royal Oak. No one knows if she rode the bike there on the 22nd of December, or whether it was placed there later.[63]

Much later in the case in 2014, Detective Williams interviewed Jerry Self, who had married Karol after she divorced Jill's dad, Tom Robinson. Williams wanted to interview Jerry separately concerning his knowledge and involvement with the Robinson family dating back to September of 1977.

Jerry told Detective Williams that he had met Karol in September of 1977 through a friend named John Mapleback who was running a New Age group out of his home in Southfield, Michigan. John led groups in the Silva Method of Mind Control Techniques. Jerry said that although the meetings were about mind control it was mainly a social gathering involving drinking, dancing, smoking and talking. He said there were normally 20-30 people at these meetings and that was how he met Karol.

John Mapleback was also an engineer that worked at Ford Motor Company.

Jerry Self said that at the time he was dating Karol she had just broken up with another guy involved in mind control named

---

63 Catherine Broad, "Oakland County Child Killer Update Meeting, April 21, 2006, OCCK Tips Final 564 pages pdf," https://catherinebroad.blog.

Ted Rodinsky. He said Ted was a "shadowy figure," adding no one really knew much about him, including Karol. Apparently Ted Rodinsky had told Karol he worked night shifts at a restaurant and then later told her he was private investigator.

After Ted was out of Karol's life in 1977 and was dating Jerry, Jerry found a Satanic Bible at Karol's house with an inscription from Ted. Jerry said he had asked Karol about it and she told him to just throw it away, which he did. Jerry mentioned that the Satanic Bible looked like it would have been very expensive.

Jerry told Detective Williams that there was a guy named Bob Thibodeau that ran a bookstore in Berkley on Woodward Ave in the '70s that Ted more than likely got the Satanic Bible from. He said that Thibodeau now owned the Mayflower Bookstore on 12 Mile Rd in Berkley. Jerry said that he and Karol were both friends with Thibodeau and had purchased books from him for years. He explained it wasn't a typical mainstream bookstore, but exclusively sold books on occult subjects, such as magic, gems, herbs, mind control...etc.

Jerry Self said that Karol still talks about how she thinks that she should have not taken Ted Rodinsky's advice on about how to handle Jill before she was murdered. He explained that Ted had told Karol to tell Jill to go outside or get away when her and Jill were arguing.

He said at that time Jill was feeling a lot of anxiety about moving to the new house in Royal Oak, and prior to her murder Karol was taking Jill to see a psychologist named Glass in Southfield.

Jerry told Detective Williams that he and Karol, months after Jill's murder, ran into Ted Rodinsky coming out of a Birmingham bookstore on Woodward. Karel point blank asked Ted if he had anything to do with Jill's murder and he said something like it was in the cards or something to that effect. He said detectives would have to ask Karol about that.

Detective Williams then joined Lieutenant Powell and Sergeant MacArthur in the process of interviewing Karol Self. Williams asked Karol about the comment Ted Rodinsky made to her at the bookstore after Jill's murder. Karol stated that when she asked Ted if he was involved in Jill's murder, Ted had said with a smug smile, "Buddha sent me."

Detective Williams had previously asked Jerry Self about the fact that Jill Robinson had told her mother months prior to her murder that she had had a premonition about being killed by a shotgun. Jerry said that according to Karol, Jill did in fact tell her that.[64]

Lieutenant Powell of the MSP expressed reservations concerning the occult angle of the case. She sent a message to Detective Tullock, also of the MSP, wondering what his thoughts were on the cult book that Jill Robinson's current husband had told them about. She thought that investigators should visit Theodore Rodinsky and check him out:

"I'm not saying it was a cult killing, but that case and circumstances are very close to home..."[65]

Tom Robinson, Jill's dad began to get angry: "I know individual officers are sparing no effort on Jill's case, but where the hell is the imaginative leadership?"

---

[64] Detective Cory Williams Narrative Report, Livonia Police Department, 128-155.
[65] Email message, Denise Powell (MSP) to Don Tullock (oakland.gov), OCCK Tips Final.

Robinson felt it was some kind of crack investigative team that virtually ignored her case and left her out in the cold. He was perplexed as to where the coordination was in the investigation and the overview of all the cases. Robinson stated that task force investigators had not been shown reports from the Troy detectives that had worked on Jill's murder.

He went on to describe the fragmentation and divisive style of the investigation:

"L. Brooks Patterson [Oakland County prosecutor] jumped on the [Kristine] Mihelich case, but I don't know where he has been on the others. He's the man who declared war on crime north of Eight Mile."[66]

Eight Mile being the dividing line between Detroit and the suburbs.

Soon after the homicide a strange individual visited the City of Royal Oak Police Department. On January 1, 1977, a Mr W.J. Connor walked into the station and began to make inquiries into the murder of Jill Robinson. He was wearing a light blue shirt, blue Air Force overcoat, a blue Air Force hat, and he was smoking a blue pipe.

This being the color suggested by Dr Bruce Danto, a psychiatrist who was involved in the investigation, as being favored by the Oakland County Child Killer. Danto had come up with a profile of the murderer.

Mr W.J. Connor was unusually curious regarding the details about the case. He asked if the bicycle [redacted] was not missed by the mother and if the bike was kept in the garage. He also wondered if the bike had a K lock on it.

---

66 "Slain Girl's Father is Angry at Police," *Detroit News*, March 27, 1977.

Since Mr Connor was so very curious, and so strangely outfitted, and so enamored with the color blue, officers ran a check on his vehicle and his activities.

Investigators noted that Mr Connor was a white male, 60 years of age, 6' tall, weighed about 180 lbs., had blue eyes and walked with a shillelagh type of cane.[67]

---

[67] Royal Oak narrative report, Detectives Meitzner and Stinson, Jill Robinson Homicide, 76-26637, December 26, 1976.

Chapter 6

Officer Flynn's Two Gun Suicide

It was said that Berkley cop Officer Christopher Flynn was deeply disturbed by the abduction and murder of Kristine Mihelich.

On April 20, 2015, Livonia Guy wrote on Catherine King Broad's blog:

"Two guns were found in Flynn's car; and Flynn's gun and a .44-caliber gun registered to Berkley Officer Krussel. The gun belonging to Krussel was found on the floor of the car between the passenger seat and door."[68]

Author Marnie Rich Keenan talked extensively to Detective Cory Williams about Officer Flynn. Williams had known Flynn for most of his life. Cory William's father and Christopher Flynn had been partners in the Berkley Police Department detective bureau during the early seventies. And Flynn's wife and William's mother worked in the same medical office at Beaumont Hospital. And the two families liked to spend vacations together.

When Christopher Flynn died in 1978, Cory Williams was sixteen. He was told by his parents that Flynn had killed himself because his wife and kids had left him and moved to West Virginia.

According to 1978 medical examiner's records, Flynn committed suicide in a church parking lot. And according to the

---

68 "McKinney," Catherine Broad,
  https://catherinebroad.blog/2015/04/20/mckinney/#comments.

medical examiner, Flynn used two guns in an attempt to shoot himself in the heart. One of the bullets, said to be a .357 caliber, was found in the back seat, and apparently went cleanly through his body without hitting anything solid. The second, a .44 caliber lead bullet, passed through multiple organs, killing him.[69]

Dr Pettinga, the medical examiner, also noted that Christopher Flynn had become deeply religious and attended church every morning. He had no drugs or alcohol in his system.[70]

Six days after Flynn died, Christopher Busch also committed suicide. He used a .22 rifle and managed to shoot himself cleanly between the eyes then tucked himself under the covers in his bed before dying.

Investigators were more than a little suspicious as to the timing of these two "suicides."

Detective Williams opened an investigation into Christopher Flynn and the circumstances surrounding his death at the behest of the King family.

After Flynn's death, OCCK task force commander, Lieutenant Robert Robertson, typed a note on the back of a tip sheet regarding Flynn. The note stated:

"Chris Flynn killed himself and he had been reported as a suspect apparently numerous times. Joe Krease, MSP, advised that he [asked] Intelligence to check him out but Intelligence has no record of this. The guys here that know him personally do not think he is involved. This tip is being closed. 12/14/78. RHR"[71]

---

69 Marnie Rich Keenan, *The Snow Killings: Inside the Oakland County Killer Investigation*, (Jefferson: Exposit), 325.
70 Rich Keenan, *The Snow Killings*, 326.
71 Ibid.

Chris Flynn had visited his daughters in West Virginia in September of 1978. He was extremely thin and they thought he was acting strange. They said he talked about becoming a monk.

During the separation with his wife Flynn was having affairs with other women. One stated that he would stare into the distance and mumble — he said he was convinced the devil was after him.

The wife of his former partner, Officer Krussel, also had some things to say. Sue Krussel said that Flynn had borrowed her husband's gun to use at the shooting range because he was involved in competitive police shooting. She also said he began stalking her and that he had told her he loved her.[72]

Allegedly failing a written test for continued detective duty, Officer Flynn was demoted from the detective bureau back to patrol duty. For a man who loved being a detective and had stated that he was the best detective in Oakland County, being demoted was truly devastating.[73]

After an extended and quite personal investigation, Detective Williams could find no evidence that Officer Flynn had any hand in the OCCK.

There was a young boy in Berkley who came forward during Christmas break in 1977 to tell the tale of what he had seen. He remembered it like it was yesterday. The snow was softly falling outside, and he wanted to ride the new bike he had gotten for Christmas. He asked his mom if he could and she had said no. But it just so happened that she got called in to work and the boy waited

---

72   Ibid., 327.
73   Ibid., 328.

until she left and gleefully took his brand-new bike out into a vacant lot where he pedaled in the snow.

He then pedaled down 12 Mile to a 7-Eleven store. As he approached the store, he saw a girl with a bag exiting the store, and right behind her a cop he recognized from his neighborhood. A few days later he saw this same girl in the newspaper stating that she had been kidnapped. Her name was Kristine Milhelich.

The boy called the OCCK hotline that was listed in the paper and the woman who answered thought he was just some smart-alec kid pranking the cops. She told him she'd come to his house if he kept it up. The boy hung up. Determined, the boy told his teacher after Christmas break what he had seen. She too thought he was making it all up. But after Tim King was killed and he brought it up again the police began to wonder.

Two cops then showed up at his school and viciously interrogated him. They took him into an empty classroom where no one could see them and accused him of lying. They pushed his head down on his desk and told him to change his story.

The boy then met a girl whose dad was a cop. The cop just happened to be Christoper Flynn. He told Officer Flynn what he had seen and how the cops had terrified him and even seemed to be stalking him now. Officer Flynn listened to his story and told him to stay home and keep his doors locked.

Five days later Officer Flynn was found dead.[74]

---

74 J. Reuben Appleman, *The Kill Jar: Obsession, Descent, and a Hunt for Detroit's Most Notorious Serial Killer*, (New York: Simon and Schuster), 198.

The .44 caliber Charter Arms that delivered the kill shot to Officer Chris Flynn was the signature gun used in the killings that Maury Terry described in *The Ultimate Evil.*

It was 1977, the new year, "Year of the Cat," and Al Stewart's titled hit of the same name climbed the charts in the early months of that year — as the killings soon would that are detailed in *The Ultimate Evil.*[75]

The police and the press acting on information from the ballistics unit from the New York Police Department, christened the murderer, "the .44-Caliber Killer," who then was subsequently known as the Son of Sam.[76]

Informants came forth to talk about the affluent people involved with the group. When Berkowitz was arrested he possessed a list of telephone numbers that were barely investigated during the original investigation.[77]

An informant also stated that a major leader of the group lived in a large mansion in either New Jersey or Long Island. And that this group was involved in drug, pornography and call girl operations involving college age girls. Shipments of illegal weapons were sometimes part of the picture and investigators knew that at least one Son of Sam murder was filmed or videotaped by the group.[78]

All of this led back to the Process, which Maury Terry and other investigators believed to have been one of the most dangerous Satanic cults in America. The Process allegedly splintered into

---

75 Maury Terry, *The Ultimate Evil, The Truth About the Cult Murders: Son of Sam and Beyond*, (New York, Barnes and Noble), 30.
76 Terry, *Ultimate Evil*, 37.
77 Ibid., 379.
78 Ibid., 379, 380.

many sub groups and has since gone underground. Like a dandelion, its seeds were carried along the winds of evil across the 1970s and into the present.

The informants explained to Terry that an alliance existed between the cult and related narcotics and pornography enterprises.

Author of *The Family*, Ed Sanders, said to Terry: "There were so many investigations going on out there after the murders that I began to wonder if the Process was a front for some intelligence operation."[79]

---

79 Ibid., 490.

Chapter 7

Helen and Hastings

John Hastings and Helen Dagner had a thing.

Helen Dagner was completely convinced John Hastings was the killer. She would often talk to the police about it. They thought she was a bit off and didn't pay any attention to her.

She wrote to the police:

You don't seem to understand...I don't want John to be the killer...he is very charming and likeable...is pleasant looking and emanates no aura of evil (so early on I was hoping against hope...that he was not the killer). However, the propensity of evidence has convinced me otherwise.

She said, "Don't you think only the killer would know little things —like Mark had no shoes— Kristine's nick name "Chris" was spelled with a Ch and not a "K," and a host of other bulleted items:

- What color and print the girl's underwear was
- What Tim had with the chicken he was fed
- The bright color patch on Chris's jeans
- That Jill struggled shortly before her death
- Tim's socks were heavy brown cotton
- Tim was carrying a basketball and skateboard
- That the bodies of more than one were in site of police stations

"And the list goes on and on…"[80]

Helen Dagner met John Hastings at her friend Sylvia's home, who was mother of his child. They lived in Alpena, Michigan.

One day Helen was at Sylvia's house and John was there. Sylvia asked her to come into the kitchen. Out of hearing range Sylvia told her she thought John could be the OCCK, or the nylon stalking rapist.

"Where'd you get that idea?" said Helen.

"One time I was standing in the kitchen, and John came up behind me," said Sylvia, "and out of the clear blue sky he says to me, I was interviewed by the Oakland County Child Killer Task Force."

Sylvia said she was so stunned that she didn't even turn around.

Then Helen asked her, "So what makes you think then he could be the nylon stalking rapist?"

"Because he has bags of nylons," she said. "And he has them in every color and in every size — panty hose, straight nylons. And he had a black pull over ski cap with the bag of nylons."

"Well, I'd like to talk to John and see what he has to say, and maybe I'll do some research on it." said Helen.

"Would you like to go for coffee with us?" said Sylvia.

They then go to the Big Boy restaurant.

We aren't even sitting there a minute when John said to Helen, "What do you know about the Oakland County Child Killer?

"I don't know anything about the Oakland County Child Killings." said Helen.

---

80 Catherine Broad, Helen Dagner OCCK Notes.

"Well, weren't you married to a cop?" said John.

"Yeah, but he never talked about the Oakland County Child Killings."

"Well, what do *you* know about the Oakland County Child Killings?" said Helen.

He explained the killer took good care of the kids. Kept them in clean clothes, and saved them from a life that would be very different than his own.

Then John said, "Well what are you going to do with your life?"

"I don't know, I guess I'm gonna write a book on serial killers."

He said "How horrible, how could you stand to be around anybody like that."

"I'm not judgmental," Helen said.

"You wanna go for coffee tonight and maybe I can help you find a serial killer."

"Sounds like a good idea to me, John."

Helen stopped at John's apartment and they went to the Big Boy restaurant. They found a seat and Helen said he was acting like he had something to tell her. He began talking about the victims of the OCCK. He knew all the schools they had attended, he knew their mother's and father's names — He knew an exceptional amount of detail.

Helen Dagner surmised he wasn't getting the information from any newspapers or TV reports.

Sometime later in the week she asked John what he thought the OCCK motive was. He explained that the killer was most likely inadequate socially, most likely couldn't get a girlfriend, and wound up doing odd jobs like washing dishes. He couldn't get a higher education and felt he was cheated out his rightful place in society.

Helen realized that in some point in the conversation that John was no longer talking in the third person or in the second person. He was talking in the first person. He was talking about himself.

At a later meeting with Helen, John began discussing his personal life. He said the family had money, but his father let the family struggle financially. He told her that he had attended an all-boys Catholic school, which made him feel more out of place. Something happened at that school. A boy was found dead, and there were rumors of sexual assault. As John told Helen this story, she felt that it was he who had been sexually assaulted.

A boy that was his friend fell of a water tower and was killed. John was present when it happened. Helen thought John might have pushed him. His emotional reaction telling the story led her to this conclusion.

John didn't go to the funeral, but his family did.

Just prior to the first OCCK murder a girlfriend that he had hoped to marry dumped him because he was broke with no prospects for earning more money.

He then started thinking about the injustice embedded in the social and financial class system, and how he was a victim of it all. Helen stated that he wanted to cause the upper class deep and permanent pain. John decided that since money could be replaced, the only way to cause this pain was to strike at the children. Besides, this was something he could do, whereas taking their money was beyond his ability.

Helen said they talked about the OCCK every day.

Then one night while they were having coffee Helen told John she was having difficulty understanding how everything was laid out, never have been in the Oakland County area. She was wondering about the body drop off sites. John then took four place mats and drew the areas.

Helen had never seen anyone draw maps like that before, so quick and so perfect. She was impressed.

The next day Helen Dagner called the Birmingham police and told them that they just had to see these maps. And they had to talk to John Hastings because it seemed he had a lot of inside information. The police said they would have to have more information to even to start to question John Hastings.

So that night she told John, "I don't think you are the killer and you have to give me some information on each of the kids that only the families and the police and the killer would know."

"Are you nuts?" he said.

And when John realized that Helen was going to leave because she wasn't taking him seriously, he said, "I put a chicken bone in Tim's pocket."

"I thought I've heard that before," said Helen.

He then listed some details pertaining to the children. Kristine had little orange or pink things on her slacks. Jill had a book in her backpack and a quarter in her pocket. One of the boys he dropped off had just rubber boots and no shoes. When he was done describing details, Helen stated that he had wound up telling her around 300 or more matches to the crimes.

Then the police started to listen to Helen Dagner's information.

They questioned John Hastings and put him through two polygraph tests. He showed the police a passport indicating when he was out of the country at the time of one of the victim's deaths.

And they let him go.

Helen Dagner said that John Hasting's passport was fake. That he had wanted to go into the "second" passport business. But according to Helen, investigators believed the passport was valid and authentic. She asked them if they had checked with other authorities who could possibly verify the passport's authenticity. They told her no.

She then asked the investigators if they had asked John where he had stayed when he was abroad. They said no.

"Did you ask him where he ate? Who he talked to?"

They said no.

"Did you check with Interpol?"

They said yes, but they couldn't confirm the information.[81]

Helen and Hastings Have Coffee and are Overheard Discussing the OCCK

Then came a man formally known as Alpena Witness (aka Bill), who heard their discussion at the Big Boy restaurant.

He described Helen Dagner as a controversial figure, was not going to win a popularity contest, hated by many people, and rather eccentric.

"But Helen was considered a pioneer in the OCCK case, and was on the Internet very early on in discussing the case. She kept

---

81 HelenDagner, OCCK Archives, Part 16,
https://www.youtube.com/watch?v=6wL6wnN_d_g.

the case alive for many years with her archives. She dedicated her life to this case." Bill said.

Bill said it was a guessing game with her. She would not always tell the truth and she was a very bitter lady, always quick to get into someone's face over something, which caused lots of arguments and fighting on the Internet.

Bill said there's no way to avoid this. Let's just get this out there right away. She had some fraud charges. She was a convicted felon. So she did spend some time in prison.

"At the end of the day I don't believe everything Helen said, and I don't believe everything the cops tell me either. And they all have the golden rule 'cover your own ass.'" Bill said.

"People are very obsessed with this case. It's a real boogie man story. People feel really like there is something in their lives that has to do with this," he said.

Bill argued about the case several times with Helen about her probably impeding people coming forward with valuable information. They even got to the point where they didn't talk for a while. And her bitterness about the whole thing had scared people off too.

Helen would only allow people to come forward with information if it was on her terms.

Bill remembered that day at the Big Boy. It was December 26, 1991.

He and his family decided to go to Alpena the day after Christmas. His kids really liked the Holiday Inn pool, so they decided to go up there.

Then he went to see an old friend who wanted to go for coffee somewhere, and they went to the Big Boy in the evening.

The waitress approached them and put some place mats on the table. She smiled and said, "You might want to hold on to these. They keep coming up missing." As she looked towards the booth in front of them.

Bill looked at the table in front of them and could see all these place mats spread on the table. The couple seated there were deep into a discussion about something. They were going over these maps. It was John Hastings and Helen Dagner, but he didn't know who they were at the time. It reminded him of getting prepared for exams, because he used to use place mats for the same thing when he went to Big Boy to study.

Bill listened to their conversation while they discussed roads, murders, and drop offs. He didn't know what a drop off was. He had never heard the term before, and didn't recognize anything being said because he didn't follow the news at the time and barely remembered the OCCK when it was news.

He thought they were cops or detectives. Then all of a sudden John Hastings mentions Troy, Michigan. Then he looked up to see what they were talking about and John had one of the maps near the edge of the table and he had a real quick glance at it. He remembered it was Interstate 75 going up the middle, and he thought it was funny because John Hastings had labeled I-75 very large and circled. And there was an X to the right. The reason Bill remembered this all so vividly was because he was working for a contract firm and he was driving to Troy on a weekly basis to pick up some things. So he knew that he definitely was talking about Troy, Michigan.

Then John said something like "I killed the children." And at some point Helen started to cry. She was facing Bill while John had his back to him. They were dressed up like they had gone to a Christmas party. Then John started saying things that shocked him.

"*I wanted to live with the children before I killed them.*" John said.

Bill said his mind tried to rationalize what he was hearing. Right away he thought, "I'm not going to believe any of this."

Bill was shocked that Helen Dagner and John Hastings were talking right in front of everybody close to the hostess stand — not off in a corner somewhere. He thought it was too surreal.[82]

John mentioned giving the children a bath. When Bill heard that he was thinking of a ritual or something, like cleaning sins or something — and wasn't even thinking forensics.

One thing that Bill thought that was particularly eerie, and totally captured his attention, was John's description about his relationship with the children. This grown man cherished "this friendship" he had with these children. He talked like he really knew the children well, like he knew the children better than the parents did. He bragged about it.

It seemed so weird to Bill...A grown man cherishing a friendship he had with these children before he killed them. He thought it was just crazy.

Bill leaned forward to hear better and at some point Helen looked right at him, and gave him this really weird look. Then John turned completely around and looked at Bill, just to see who Helen was looking at. There was a staring contest there for a second, Bill said. Then Bill just kind of looked away until John turned back

---

[82] Andy Berthiaume podcast, November 2018, "Alpena Witness," 1st segment, https://catherinebroad.blog/2020/09/22/alpena-witness/.

around. But that bothered Bill too, because John knew he was there, and he was still talking about these murders.

The waitress came and filled their coffees, and John was still talking about the OCCK stuff like he's talking about the weather. All the emotion he put into it — did this guy rehearse this? Bill started to look around, and wondered if anyone else was noticing John and Helen talking.

Bill said that John talked about Tim and Jill the most.

At one point John play acted like he was holding a gun and said, "I shot her in the head. In the snow."

John talked about a room upstairs, where he would watch TV and play games with the children.

And that John said that he lived next door to his parents.

Bill said he had a front seat to this drama, but he had buried it in his memory.[83]

He didn't discover anything about Helen Dagner, or her story, until thirteen years later. In 2004 the BTK killer (acronym for bind, torture, kill) topic was popular, and he was reading up on it. Then he saw a thread written by someone called "Helen and Mystic" about this person named John, who thought the BTK killer could be tied to the OCCK. Then Bill saw Alpena, Michigan, being mentioned in the forum, along with Big Boy and child murders.

Bill started having flashbacks. The first thing he remembered was Helen looking at him with that really weird look. Then it all started coming back to him, and he was totally stunned.

The first thing he did was read all he could to get a fix on the OCCK. Bill wrote to Helen, and told her that he was there.

---

83 Berthiaume, "Alpena," Ibid., 2nd segment.

"People read murder mystery novels, and I wake up and I find I'm in the middle of one," Bill said.

Helen said, "Either you're John, or you were there."

Bill said that he and Helen corresponded after that for quite a few years.

Bill decided that John Hastings at least had a fantasy about killing these children. But a lot of information that John divulged concerning the child killings was not accurate either.

"In my book he's still a suspect." Bill said. "And the reason why is he has never told the truth. He denied telling Helen any of this. He denied it in '92 when they investigated him. And he denied it in 2008 when they investigated him again. These polygraphs? They don't mean crap."

The first law enforcement person Bill talked to was his cop neighbor in Roseville. Michigan. He told him to go talk to detectives, they'll wanna hear about it.

At the end of 2004 Bill went to the closest police station and told them that he had some possible information on the OCCK, and they gave him some numbers to call. He was then bounced around to various police departments. In 2005 Bill talked to a guy in Pontiac who was responsible for the case before the MSP took over the files. He told the police contact what he had witnessed in Alpena at the Big Boy. The police officer said, "Does this have to do with Helen Dagner?" And Bill told him that it did. Then the police officer told him that Helen Dagner had fabricated the whole thing, and that John was from a respectable family, and there was no way he had heard those discussions. He would have had to have heard some other discussion. But he could still come in and fill out a police report if he wanted.

Bill said he got off the phone thinking, "What am I getting into here?" He knew what he had heard at Big Boy.

Bill reached out to another cop from Alpena which he had known since he was little. They started out with small talk and finally Bill mentioned Helen Dagner, just to see what he would say and right away he mentioned that she had these fraud charges. Bill mentioned Big Boy and parts of the discussion he had heard. He asked him what he should do. He said you really ought to talk to the people that came to town to investigate that in the early '90s.

Bill then talked to a detective from Birmingham. Right up front Bill told him he had heard these discussions, and could verify that they really had taken place. The officer said, "I know. I interviewed the Big Boy staff." Bill said his wife used to work at Big Boy, and asked him who he had talked to at the restaurant, and he didn't remember, or didn't want to say. The officer then said John was not a priority, and he wasn't a top suspect, but they had a whole "boatload" of suspects.

Bill was angry that it was a whole complete line of bull they had told him and his wife.[84]

Bill said that detectives never interviewed any staff at Big Boy, and because of what they had told them, he and his wife decided to take another trip to Alpena to find out who they talked to — who they interviewed at the Big Boy.

He called a news hotline and got an answering machine — Channel 4 possibly. Then after Bill had called this hotline there was a newscast about "details of a bogus confession." But they had never called Bill back, and had never talked to him concerning his information.

---

84 Ibid., 3rd segment.

MSP took over the files, and Bill had tried to contact them also. He had talked to officials there and they didn't want to meet with him. The person he talked to asked if he was nuts. Bill said, "Not the last time I checked."

Then Bill talked to a Livonia detective. And this detective was the only one who sat down with him and really listened to his information. Bill felt that he was the only cop who asked the right questions and was interested in the case.

He then contacted Barry King. He said that Barry was firm on the fact that John was cleared. Bill mentioned that if it wasn't for the King family the public would be completely in the dark about the case.

"You have a controversial figure, Helen Dagner, known by some as a crackpot in town," Bill said. "She had a relationship with a cop. It was a soap opera and a train wreck ready to happen, even before John came on to the scene. So then you have something as ridiculous as a murder confession at a Big Boy restaurant in Alpena, Michigan."

Then there was the fake passport issue. Helen claimed John had a fake passport, and he was out of town for one murder. The police did their own FOIA on the passport to determine if it was authentic or not.

A detective from Birmingham said John was being watched in Colorado. According to Helen, the detective in Birmingham was watching the wrong John in Colorado, and may have cleared him because of that. She said John had never lived in Colorado.

John's address was very close to the Busch residence. They lived about a block away from each other. The cops went to John's house to question him about Christopher Busch, who he denied knowing.

John still denied telling people that he told Helen he was the OCCK, but he had to admit to drawing the maps. It would have been difficult for him to deny that.

On *America's Most Wanted* website, John's family was on the forum there trying to defend John. John's sister said that John was educating Helen about the case. And that John had read a lot about crime and was trying to discuss it with her and she had made all this up that he was the killer. Then Bill wrote on the forum that he was there and heard some of these stories. He said if at least John would have admitted to saying what he said the night he was there at the Big Boy he wouldn't have gotten involved like he did. But because John denied it, and because Bill felt so strongly that was wrong, for the victim's families he got involved.

When they went to interview him in Georgia, John came to the interview with a crime encyclopedia. It was kind of set it up like John's sister was describing about John educating Helen on the case. The detective from Livonia also thought it was really bizarre, that John would bring this crime book.

Bill said that the one thing that Helen always said was, *"If they're not looking at John, they're not going to solve the case."*

Bill told Helen that John just might have been a story teller. Helen got mad that he wouldn't see her point of view that John was the killer.

But Bill couldn't get over the fact that John looked a lot like the sketch. Some people thought the composite sketches looked like Greg Greene, Busch's accomplice, but he would have to have been out of prison because that's when those composites were drawn and in the public eye. The detective from Livonia said Greene was definitely in the county jail at the time of King's abduction and murder.[85]

A Polygraph in Georgia

Detective Sergeant Gary Gray of the MSP and Detective Cory Williams of the Livonia Police Department traveled to Atlanta, Georgia to interview John Hastings and to ask if he would take a polygraph in order to clear himself once and for all of all of the child killings. He agreed.

On October 6, 2009, OCCK suspect John Hastings was scheduled to undergo a polygraph by Steve Duncan of the Georgia Highway Patrol. When Hastings arrived for the test he was upset and agitated. He made a big deal of the four polygraph questions that Detectives Gray and Williams told him he would have to answer. Hastings said that they had lied to him.

Steve Duncan explained to John Hastings that the examination had to do with him and the test was needed in order to clear him. Duncan then read Hastings his Miranda rights and then had no further problem with John Hastings.

Georgia polygraphs involved separate tests for each victim. On the third test involving Kristine Mihelich, John Hastings exhibited a pronounced and debilitating response to this exam; appearing exhausted and unable to continue.

After the polygraphs were given, Duncan took a break to score the results. He then confronted John Hastings with the results of the tests. Duncan observed that John Hastings never denied anything he confronted him with evidence of his guilt and just sat

---

85 Ibid., 4th segment.

there and listened as though he had resigned himself to the fact that he was in fact involved in some way with the child killings. But then he seemed to rally himself and started to deny the results of the polygraphs.

Steve Duncan stated that during the polygraphy process, John Hastings made some very strange statements to him, stating more than once, "I can't tell you," then John would stop and follow up that statement by saying, "Because that's not the truth."

Steve Duncan told Detectives Gray and Williams that he and his supervisor who had also witnessed the entire examination process were so convinced that John Hastings was somehow involved in the child killings that if Hastings were to confess his involvement, they already had a plan in place where they would hold him for officers in Michigan to obtain a warrant. He emphasized that they were that convinced.

Duncan reiterated that there was no question in his mind that John Hastings had some type of involvement with the child killings. He said that he didn't know to what degree of involvement he might have had, whether through knowledge of the killings, assisting with the murders, or committing the murders himself, he firmly believed that he was involved in some way.

Steve Duncan was asked by Michigan detectives if John Hastings knew suspects Christopher Busch and Gregory Greene. Duncan stated that John Hastings did mention Christopher Busch and that he committed suicide. When asked if he thought that John Hastings knew Christopher Busch, Steve Duncan replied absolutely.[86]

---

86 Oakland County Child Killer Investigation, Georgia Highway Patrol/Polygraph, Michigan Department of State Police, Supplemental

On January 29, 2021 Catherine King Broad addressed a FOIA request to the Georgia Highway Patrol to obtain John Hastings polygraph information conducted by Steve Duncan. It was her understanding that Steve Duncan had forwarded copies of all the DVDs of the polygraphs, the three separate reports of three victims, and pre and post interview information from the Hastings polygraphs to the MSP.

She stated that she knew the MSP had buried the information regarding the fact that the Georgia Highway Patrol were convinced that John Hastings had involvement with the murders and that they had a plan ready to hold him for officers in Michigan to obtain a warrant. She further elaborated that they withheld this information from Detective Cory Williams and emphasized that time was of the essence because John Hastings was still alive and quite possibly involved in the homicides.[87]

She then wrote to Colonel Joseph Gasper, Director of the MSP, addressing the fact that the agency told her that they could not locate copies of the DVD or separate reports prepared by Georgia State Highway polygrapher Steve Duncan and emphasized that the OCCK is an open serial homicide case and materials pertaining to the case should be easily accessible.

Catherine King Broad forwarded everything in her Georgia State Highway FOIA request to Colonel Gasper, and added more information regarding John Hastings. She stated that John Hastings was a neighbor of suspect Christopher Busch and was the same age as Busch and was named by a living witness who spoke with a MSP

Incident Report, October 9, 2009, Catherine Broad, https://catherinebroad.blog/2021/01/13/john-hastings/.
87 Georgia Open Records Request, Catherine Broad, https://catherinebroad.blog/2021/04/28/john-hastings-2/.

detective as a "hanger on" with Christopher Busch, and as a "child hunter" for the pedophile ring operating in Oakland and Wayne Counties. She stated that despite Duncan's conclusions of John Hastings likely involvement in the child killings documented in the materials that MSP claimed couldn't be found, no one had followed up on John Hastings even though he is still alive. She stressed that the time to lean on Hastings would have been back in October of 2009 as suggested by Steve Duncan, and a competent detective could still get valuable information from interrogating him and his family.

She wrote that more importantly the MSP could not have it both ways. They couldn't claim it was an open case by protecting records in the case; then pretending to honor any FOIA request concerning the OCCK, and then state publicly that the agency is losing documents and other materials directly related to the investigation, clearly doing nothing to advance the clearing of the case regarding publicly accessible information.

She argued that it is long past time for a court ruling that the OCCK investigation is no longer an open case so the MSP cannot continue to hide information from the public by arguing that it is a "pending case" or "ongoing investigation." Broad stated that it is the burden of the agency to show exactly how disclosure would harm a law enforcement proceeding, indicating that the MSP would not even circle back to John Hastings *after* using the services of a polygrapher from the Georgia Highway Patrol, or attempt to substantiate any information given by living victims in recent years regarding the case.

Catherine King Broad ended the letter by stating that FOIA was designed to allow people knowledge and insight into how the government does business by the information it collects. She said that the MSP's FOIA response certainly provides that kind of insight.[88]

Detective Williams later divulged his frustration with the fact that he was thrown off the OCCK task force by Detective Gray of the MSP in 2009 for talking to Helen Dagner, while all along Gray was talking with her. Detective Williams stated that he was questioning Helen Dagner's information about John Hastings with Gray before the interview in Georgia. Williams expressed his surprise and dismay that Gray was sharing what they were working on, had lied to him, and had withheld valuable information concerning other leads.[89]

---

88 FOIA Appeal, Catherine Broad, https://catherinebroad.blog/2021/05/26/foia-appeal/.
89 Cory W., Comments, "More," Catherine Broad, https://catherinebroad.blog/2023/08/27/more-5/.

Chapter 8

Doug Wilson Knows the Car

The Blue Gremlin in the OCCK case was a red herring. Someone saw Timothy King talking to someone in what they thought was a Blue Gremlin. And thus the urban legend of the Blue Gremlin. The press picked this up and ran with it. It became embedded in the public consciousness — somehow this car was involved with the abduction of Tim King.

And then something happened. It was one of those strange coincidences of the OCCK case. If Barry King had not married his second wife Janice, he would never have found a very pertinent piece of information related to the case.

Janice told him about a guy who had worked in the car design business with her deceased husband. His name was Doug Wilson and he had a story to tell. He said he was up at the same store that Tim was the night he was kidnapped. He saw Tim with an old man and a young man. The FBI asked him if he was willing to be hypnotized; he said sure.

Doug Wilson saw a LeMans there at the market. Not a Blue Gremlin. He gave investigators a load of detailed information.[90]

Lieutenant Kalbfleisch transported Doug Wilson to the office of Dr Rossi, on June 1, 1977, to undergo hypnosis by the

---

[90] "Chapter Title: 24. Prosecutor Disclosures," Decades of Deceit: A True Story of the King Family Search for the Oakland County Child Killer.

doctor. Wilson then began to tell his story. Under hypnosis Wilson indicated that he parked his red Alfa Romeo at the rear of Chatham Market. He then observed a young boy riding a skateboard down the parking lot. He said the boy appeared to be about seven or eight years of age and was very small. Wilson said he remembered the boy was wearing blue pants and tennis shoes. And he remembered a jacket, and something about stripes.

The boy jumped off the skateboard as he approached the back wall of Chatham market and the skate board ran into the wall. Then Wilson saw a white male, approximately thirty years of age, 5'10 to 6'0, with dark hair going down to the nape of his neck and partially covering his ears. The man had dark eyebrows and was wearing casual clothes. Doug Wilson could only remember the jacket this individual was wearing — a brown jacket, light weight, smooth — possibly a wind breaker. He thought it could have been the boy's father watching him on the skateboard.

After getting out his car and locking it, Wilson saw another man in a car who appeared to be watching the boy on the skateboard. Wilson said the car was American made and it wasn't a Chrysler. He thought it could be a Cutlass, and that it was one color. He thought it was an intermediate size car.

Doug Wilson observed the license plate number of the car. He then made up a little mnemonic jingle to remember it just in case on the off chance it hit his car. One license plate number he came up with was GBR-222, which was GERBER 222 to remember the number. The other letter/number combination he remembered was GJR-222.

That was all the information he could provide during the first interview with Dr Rossi. Due to time constraints another hypnosis session was scheduled.

On June 9, 1977 Doug Wilson was again put under hypnosis. He described the men he saw in the parking lot and a sketch artist made drawings of his observations.

Wilson stated that he felt that the two men he observed were together for the purpose of abducting this boy.[91]

In 2013 Doug Wilson gave an interview to a Detroit area news channel and told them all about his FBI hypnosis sessions. He said that he thought that his information would be utilized during that time period to apprehend the killer(s). As Catherine King Broad points out on her website, the reason that the police didn't go public with any of this very detailed and valuable information was because, "They did not want to alert the owner of the LeMans."

Catherine goes on to explain that what is so important about Doug Wilson's statement is not that he saw a TV show about prolific serial killer John Wayne Gacy many years after the murders and thought it looked like the man he saw sitting in the car near where a younger man was talking to Tim, but that the FBI never acted on the information.

Gacy was born in 1942 and would have been 35 in March of 1977. He therefore would have appeared similar in appearance to the composite picture made by the sketch artist.

Barry King managed to track down Doug Wilson in 2012 and have an extended discussion with him.

Wilson said the reason he remembered the specific model was because he was a car designer for Chrysler and the LeMans was one of his least favorite designs. He said that the process of hypnosis was very powerful, so much so that he could remember

---

91 Doug Wilson Hypnosis Session with Dr Rossi, Narrative Report, Lieutenant Kalbfleisch, Interviews.

and envision specific details that his conscious mind did not register or imprint at the time. Wilson was very definitive on the blue/green color. When they took him back to scrape the brick wall for residue from the skateboard hitting the wall, he was even able to count the bricks and point to where the skateboard most likely hit and they then found a spot where pieces of the orange neoprene of Tim's skateboard had been imprinted onto the wall.

Doug Wilson said he saw the LeMans again with the 222 license plate drive by his home when he was mowing his lawn.

Wilson moved to California in 1982 and assumed that the police had followed up on his information and that the families of the victims had also been kept up to speed concerning his part in the investigation. He said he was shocked when Barry King called and said this was the first time he was hearing about his hypnosis session with the FBI and what was uncovered. He then tried in vain to remember the two FBI agents, stating that they were about his age at the time.

Catherine King Broad felt that it was a deliberate cover-up of the LeMans information. She said it was only one of a few examples of this LeMans info being deep-sixed by the FBI as well as the MSP.

At that point in time the FBI had not responded to the King family FOIA request on the Wilson information.[92]

When the FBI did finally send the documents to the King family, they consisted of 12 pages of news articles relating to the abduction of Tim King and a very strange short story. It was from *Good Housekeeping* magazine entitled, "Linda's Haunting Vision."

---

92 Catherine Broad, "Thank you Doug Wilson," https://catherinebroad.blog/2013/02/04/thank-you-doug-wilson/.

The FBI did not relay how this related to the OCCK case or the interviews and hypnosis sessions of Doug Wilson.[93]

It should be noted that the correspondence of Doug Wilson and Barry King in 2012 is very different from the information that Lieutenant Kalbfleisch had transcribed concerning the hypnosis sessions.

Wilson sent an email to Barry King describing the incident. He stated that the young man talking to Tim was wearing a plaid shirt jacket and jeans, and was also wearing a baseball cap over his shoulder length hair. Wilson also described a man in a car who fixed his gaze on him and stared at him intently as he walked by his car and towards the market. Wilson felt a bit unnerved and thought he might be a car thief. He described him as being around 55-65 years of age, and added that his hair was totally gray and he was about 20-30 pounds overweight with a very round face.

He said the make of the car was a 1973 Pontiac LeMans 2-door coupe. This observation was not mentioned in the Kalbfleisch transcript.

Wilson continued into the store and came out 15-20 minutes later. Everyone at that point in time was gone —the boy, the young man, and the older man sitting in the car.

Doug Wilson had not been paying attention to the news concerning the abductions of the kids in the area. He stated that if he had he would have been more suspicious of the situation

---

93 Catherine Broad, "From the FBI FOIA response re: documents relating to witness Doug Wilson's statements in the OCCK investigation," https://catherinebroad.blog/2013/05/24/from-the-fbi-foia-response-re-documents-relating-to-witness-doug-wilsons-statements-in-the-occk-investigation/.

regarding the boy and the two men. The only thing that concerned him at that time was possible theft or damage to his new car. All he had observed in the parking lot was totally forgotten when he got into his new Alfa Romeo and returned home.

He described the hypnosis session being conducted at the University of Michigan campus. In attendance were the two agents, a sketch artist, and the psychiatrist who would hypnotize him. When he was put under hypnosis he wondered if he really was hypnotized. Wilson remembers feeling totally aware of what was around him.

But what had escaped him was the time.

When the session had ended, he thought maybe only 15-20 minutes had elapsed, but glancing at his watch was shocked to see that 4 hours had passed.

The investigators were very excited about his information. He was able to confirm the speculations of the FBI that two men were involved. Wilson said that the sketch artist was able to get a pretty good likeness of each man. But he stated that the most important information to him was his identification of the car the older man was sitting in — a 1973 LeMans 2-door coupe.

Doug Wilson then discovered that the investigators already knew about the make of the car. When Kristine Mihelich had been dropped off the car had backed into a snow bank and left a perfect impression of the car's rear bumper.[94]

Wilson also had observed that the older man sitting in the car resembled John Wayne Gacy, the serial killer. And he had mentioned this to Barry King in his email correspondence.

---

94 Catherine Broad, "From the FBI FOIA response."

Apparently Gacy resembled another person closely involved in the OCCK case.

When Author Marnie Rich Keenan obtained the FOIA file on Bloomfield Township Police Department Corporal Richard McNamee, and showed it to Catherine King Broad, they both were surprised at the resemblance between the two men. They of course were instantly reminded of the statement made by witness Doug Wilson.

Corporal Richard McNamee was the officer who responded to the Christopher Busch "suicide" scene. McNamee was called by Charles Busch, who was called by the maid who was suspicious after finding too many papers laying around the house entryway.[95]

---

95 Catherine Broad, "Who Looks Most Like John Wayne Gacy?," https://catherinebroad.blog/2020/08/29/who-looks-most-like-john-wayne-gacy/.

Chapter 9

Man About Town, Arch Sloan

Archibald Edward Sloan knew a lot of people. Most people called him Arch. He was/is a suspect in the OCCK case. Investigators wondered if he didn't kill the kids outright or had dropped off their bodies, and then concealed the evidence regarding the body drop vehicles. Or all three.

He and his family originally hailed from Pennsylvania. Where he had brought with him a long rap sheet of molesting kids and other nefarious deeds. There was a trial held there in the Commonwealth of Pennsylvania, County of Washington, for sodomy and assault, and solicitation to commit sodomy concerning one Archibald Sloan.

During the trial the prosecutor asked the child victim some questions:
Q. I also understand you to say the reason you didn't tell anybody about this on March 13th, was because you were afraid of Mr Sloan?
A. Yes.
Q. What were you afraid that he was going to do?
A. Kill me.[96]

---

[96] Commonwealth of Pennsylvania vs Arch Sloan, Sodomy Section 501 and the Solicitation to Commit Sodomy 502, (Court of Common Pleas), Catherine Broad, https://catherinebroad.blog/2021/12/06/sloans-deviant-days-in-pennsylvania/.

And so it went for Arch Sloan. He is serving a life sentence for the rape of boys in 1983 in a Michigan penitentiary. Sloan has been interrogated, interviewed, and offered deals, but gave nothing substantial to investigators regarding the OCCK case.

Sloan was named early on in the investigation as a suspect in the murder of Mark Stebbins.[97]

Apparently MSP Officer Dave Robertson was so concerned with what Arch Sloan knew, or who he could implicate, that he specifically stated that no one was to interview Sloan and if someone tried, he personally was to be told immediately.[98]

Some investigators came to visit Arch Sloan in prison and they brought with them a psychiatrist, Larry Simon. Detective Miller explained that he and Larry had discussed various cases throughout the years and Miller told Larry Simon about this one and they wanted to find out what direction they should take regarding the case. They spent a long time talking. Many transcribed pages worth. Sloan emphasized how he could not kill anything or anyone; how he had problems skinning a deer.

Mr Simon: Let's put it this way, what would you do if you were the killer's therapist or guardian angel, if you had one chance to stop a potential killer from killing any kids in the future...what would be your—"

Mr. Sloan: I have news for you, when it comes to preservation of a kid or anyone in your life there is no patient/doctor relationship, I don't give a fuck what they say and if they come

---

97 Catherine Broad, "Mark Douglas Stebbins," https://catherinebroad.blog/2024/02/15/mark-douglas-stebbins/.
98 Catherine Broad, Comments, "Sloan's deviant days in Pennsylvania," https://catherinebroad.blog/2021/12/06/sloans-deviant-days-in-pennsylvania/.

down to the point where I either blow his ass away or walk out the door, I'm going to blow him away.

Arch Sloan went on to explain. Some of the smartest people are in prison he said. But, he added, there was more to it. You had to be lucky.[99]

He also said whoever committed the crime was extremely lucky.

Mr Simon: Why lucky?

Mr Sloan: To be able to get away with what he got away with and nobody seen him. He was invisible. Why was he invisible? What kind of job did he have that he could be invisible? Who—

Mr Simon: What do you think?

Mr Sloan: Who is invisible that we don't pay attention to, firemen, policemen, (inaudible), power company guys, telephone people....[100]

Perhaps inadvertently Arch Sloan had given up the plot. Arch Sloan drove a tow truck. Blending in was easy. No one paid attention to tow truck drivers. Detective Williams would bring up this point later.

Mr Simon: Let me ask you this, you mentioned the fact that there was a service call in the area where Mark Stebbins was — [101]

Mr Sloan: Right, I was on the north side of 94, the expressway, Powers Road, just earlier that morning.

Mr Simon: Allegedly what you said is if you were 20 minutes earlier you, quote —

Mr Sloan: I might have seen — caught that son of a bitch, might have seen it because the expressway is like this. Like I said,

---

99 Videotaped Interview of Edward Sloan, May 17, 2012, 74.
100 Videotaped Interview, 91.
101 Ibid., 90.

I don't know if Powers Road goes straight through or not and I was there servicing a car, okay, and that's the only thing I recollect was there at that (inaudible) the car and you could see across, there's no trees or nothing, okay, that's what I meant, I would have probably caught the son of a bitch, seen what kind of car it was or what's going on there because if you see somebody doing something stopped on the side of the road you look.

Mr Simon: You said 20 minutes —

Mr Sloan: The time they said it happened and I said if I would have been 20 minutes earlier, I said I might have caught him; I might have.

Mr Simon: Who told you that?

Mr Sloan: The police did.

Mr Simon: Okay.

Mr Sloan: The police did when they was questioning me and everything else.[102]

This tow truck being in the vicinity of a body drop concerning Arch Sloan would come up again during the murder and subsequent body drop of Timothy King. Detective Williams would question Sloan regarding this.

Then there was the question of evidence.

Mr Sloan: Supposedly that's what got me in all this fucking trouble in here, they said they found shit in my car, blah, blah, blah. My car wasn't involved in it as far as I know of. Other than me and my little brother and Bobby, maybe one of my sisters because I bought it from one of my baby sisters.[103]

---

102 Ibid., 172.
103 Ibid., 173.

Arch Sloan was perplexed as to how evidence got into his truck that he knew nothing about.

Mr Sloan: You know, I don't know where they found what they found or whatever but I'm trying to figure out how something could get in my trunk that I had nothing to do with.[104]

Investigators from the MSP assured Arch Sloan that they were there to be completely truthful with him, but in order to keep the integrity of the investigation intact there were things that they couldn't divulge. They said they would be tape recording everything for their protection and his.

Arch Sloan understood. He began discussing various types of communication equipment with the investigators.

Ms Powell: What did you carry one for, when you were in __[105]

Mr Sloan: No, I carried a small Motorola when I worked for the wrecker service. I was on call 24/7.

Ms Powell: You had a recorder or —

Mr Sloan: No. No, I had a — my sister worked for Rockwell International and they give their employees a bunch of perks, whatever you want to call them, you know, and she'd give it to me as a present and we used to use it with the — having fun with it, recording what somebody said, catch them trying to say something stupid, look what you said and this guy Bill was a friend of my dad's that hunted with him up north and he would snore and sometimes he would sound like he was running a chainsaw and hit a pine knot and he'd stop and start back up again.

---

104 Ibid., 179.
105 Tape Recorded Interview of Edward Sloan, May 10, 2012, 4.

Mr Sloan: So I got the little recorder going and Richard Clayton, who was a Detroit police officer, spoke, my dad spoke, he spoke, the others spoke and I spoke...[106]

Investigators began showing photographs of people that Sloan had associated with in the past that were implicated in the OCCK case.

Mr Sloan: That's Mr. Clayton and I think this is up north at — because that looks like —

Then things started getting a little fuzzy. Arch Sloan wasn't sure if it was Mr Clayton or his dad.

Mr Sloan: I think that's Mr Clayton but I'm not positive, because of the coloration it's kind of hard to —

Ms Powell: It's an older picture.

Mr Sloan: It might even be my dad.

Ms Powell: It think it — yeah, it did look like your dad but we weren't sure.

Mr Tullock: I wasn't sure either.

Arch Sloan had no problem identifying people in photographs after that mix up between the Detroit Police Officer and his father.

Mr Sloan: My mom used to take all the pictures and I got it from her because I got a camera when I was fourth grade I think, Ronnie Hawkeye. In fact I have pictures of her on her first birthday, this is my sister Joyce, and mom always made scratch cakes icing, the sticky stuff, you know?[107]

Ms Powell: Uh-huh.

---

106 Tape Recorded Interview of Edward Sloan, 9.
107 Ibid., 10.

Mr Sloan: Dad would come in and they blew out the candles and dad put her back in the high chair and says she gets first piece and she had icing everywhere and I had pictures. That's myself, my brother Lee, my brother Robert, my brother Joseph, Dawna, my baby sister Joyce, my middle sister Jan and mom.[108]

MSP Investigators seem to have made up their minds as to the innocence of Arch Sloan.

Mr Tullock: There are certain areas that we wanted to after our last conversation just kind of clarify with you and I'll even be candid kind of like we were last time, most of these areas go to try to develop additional information and support you being adamant I'm not involved, I'm not involved, I think you guys are on the wrong track here so, you know, our demeanor is a little different personalities, meaning Denise and I are the same personalities but it may be different demeanor personalities than other investigators and we're not going to defend them, we're not going to explain it, you form your opinion and we'll form ours.[109]

MSP investigators were hinting at "the other investigators" being those not in sync with their investigation. Perhaps referring to Wayne County investigators, which was an issue that would come up time and time again.

Mr Tullock: As you know we are going to do things technically correct and I know you've dealt with a lot of other investigators in the past, everybody has different ways, some people are, you know, louder and that's not productive for a person that's cooperating and we don't operate that way.[110]

---

108 Ibid., 12.
109 Ibid., 13,14.
110 Ibid., 16,17.

Maybe Arch Sloan caught the hint. He realized that some of the investigators didn't consider him such a high priority anymore. He was no longer a deer in the headlights.

Mr Sloan: You're not going to be...be satisfied...let's put it this way, you're not going to be satisfied until the real person is caught and until such time, I'm still a person of interest. I'm not at the top of the list anymore but still a person of interest.
Mr Tullock: Thank you for having that intellect.[111]

Detective Cory Williams got a call. It was from Detective McPhee, who said he had listened to an interview of Detroit Police Department Sergeant Richard Clayton who was friends with Arch Sloan. Richard Clayton was describing the El Rancho Farm property in Montmorency County as being his family's property. But then during this Detroit Police Department Internal Affairs interview, Clayton became uncooperative. He did not want to talk about Arch Sloan. Especially when they tried to get information from him concerning Sloan's whereabouts.[112]

It seems that the MSP had to turn over evidence (documents) that had been requested via subpoena to the 3rd Circuit Grand Jury, which had been convened in the matter of the homicide of Timothy King. This Grand Jury was authorized in September of 2010 by 3rd Circuit Chief Virgil Smith, at the request of Prosecutor Kim Worthy. Assistant Prosecuting Attorney Robert Moran and Detective Williams accompanied Prosecutor Worthy to this meeting with Chief Judge Smith. Judge Smith agreed with the

---
111 Ibid., 6.
112 Ibid., 17.

request for a Grand Jury investigation in this case and appointed Circuit Court Judge Timothy Kenny as the "One Man Grand Jury."

MSP Colonel Eddie Washington, Captain Harold Love, and Detective/Sergeant Dave Robertson were then subpoenaed and appeared to testify in front of the Grand Jury. They were also requested to provide document evidence connected to a lead Wayne County investigators were working on involving the death of Tim King. The above stated witnesses also provided testimony about how this lead developed from mitochondrial DNA, which was produced from hair found back in the spring of 2009.[113]

In January/February of 2010, Wayne County Investigators had received information that the MSP might have a DNA match in the OCCK case. Then in August and September of 2010, Chief Robert Stevenson of Livonia Police Department confirmed through conversations with Captain Love and Colonel Washington, that their agency did in fact have a DNA match in the OCCK case connected to a suspect in prison on the west side of the state of Michigan. It was then revealed to detectives that this DNA match was a match to hairs found on the bodies of the fourth victim, Timothy King, and the first victim, Mark Stebbins.

MSP explained that the suspect's hairs were removed from a vehicle in Southfield during a traffic stop during the original investigation and came back a match to the suspect who was currently in prison. The suspect was not the registered owner of the vehicle that the hairs were removed from. The MSP wouldn't reveal the identify of the suspect to the Livonia Police.

---

[113] Wayne County Prosecutor's Office Grand Jury investigation, The Homicide of Timothy King, Body found in Livonia in 1977, Reporting Officer: Detective Cory M. Williams (WCPO), October 2010, 9.

During the Grand Jury proceedings on October 26, 2010, this name came up. It was Arch Edward Sloan.

The MSP had received confirmation from the FBI Lab in Quantico, Virginia, back in January of 2010, that there was a mitochondrial DNA match to hairs from Mark Stebbins and Timothy King. The hairs from the two victims matched a hair submitted by the MSP in the fall of 2009. These would have been the hairs on glass slides thought at first to be animal hairs, which were later determined to be human hairs.

These hairs were finally located in 2009, along with the original lab log book from the initial investigation, after a lot of pressure from Detective Williams and FBI Special Agent John Oulette. The items were located after many searches of storage facilities and labs through the years.

Detective Williams remembered this. He was in the storage facility when the slides were located and determined to contain human hairs. He remembered that the slides were initially marked as fur, dirt, or debris. He also remembered that MSP forensic scientist Lori Bruski said that the slides needed to be sent to the FBI Lab in Quantico for mitochondrial comparison.[114]

On October 27, 2010, Detective Williams started his investigation into suspect Arch Sloan.[115]

Detective Williams discovered that in January of 2010, the MSP received a report from the FBI Lab in Quantico stating that the hairs found on the bodies of King and Stebbins matched the hairs taken from a Pontiac vehicle during the original investigation in the 1970s. The Pontiac was driven by Arch Sloan and a suspect

---

[114] Wayne County Prosecutor's Office, Detective Williams, 1.
[115] Ibid.

named John Crosbie, who was a friend of Ruth Stebbins, victim Mark Stebbins's mother. The MSP must have had a report or notes indicating that the Pontiac was driven by or connected to Arch Sloan and/or John Crosbie. That meant when all the agencies and information connected to the OCCK investigation was brought to the Oakland County Prosecutors Office and scrutinized, MSP and Oakland County Prosecutors had all this information, but shared none of it.

They had lied to Prosecutor Worthy and all the Oakland and Wayne County Chiefs of Police that were there along with many investigators, saying that what they presented that day was current information regarding the case and there was no new evidence. They said nothing about a DNA match.

On further review of the lab reports, Assistant Prosecutor Moran and Detective Williams discovered that MSP had buccal swabbed Arch Sloan and a relative of John Crosbie and compared the results to the hair removed from the Pontiac. The FBI then sent a lab report to MSP in the summer of 2010 indicating that neither Crosbie nor Sloan matched the hair from King and Stebbins that was removed from the Pontiac. Detective Williams deduced that the suspect had access to the Pontiac vehicle and more than likely knew and/or associated with Sloan and/or Crosbie. Williams also surmised that Sloan and/or Crosbie could very well still be the killers.[116]

John Crosbie's name surfaced early in the Mark Stebbins investigation.

On February 15, 1976, the day of the disappearance of Mark Stebbins, John Crosbie was present at the American Legion Hall,

---

116 Ibid., 2.

located at 1741 Livernois, Ferndale. It was said that John Crosbie offered to drive Mark home when his mother, Ruth Stebbins, gave him permission to leave. Mark declined the offer and walked home alone.[117]

It was known to authorities that John Crosbie was a close associate of a sex offender of minor children.

A search warrant affidavit was then drawn up for the search of John Crosbie's vehicle. The items listed in the warrant pertained to the condition of the body or items found on the body:

1. That the remains of Mark Douglas Stebbins were found in a crouched, folded position indicating being confined in a small area, like the trunk of a car.

2. Hairs were present on the exterior of the clothing.

3. An officer of the Ferndale Police Department had observed the body of the victim and how it appeared as if in a cramped, folded position. He also observed silver gray hair on the clothing of the victim, and stated that the owner of the 1965 Chevrolet, John Crosbie, did have a cat that was gray in color.[118]

After staking out his house, the officer observed John Crosbie pulling into the driveway of his residence. Crosby exited the car, carrying a box. The officer then radioed the police station that the subject was back. Back-up arrived, and officers apprehended Cosbie.

When they arrived at the station, they observed what appeared to be strands of light brown or blond hair caught on a rear hinge of the cooler.[119]

---

117 Ibid., 3.
118 Affidavit for Search Warrant, State of Michigan, Oakland County, Lieutenant Detective Patrick T. Sullivan, February 19, 1976.
119 Affidavit for Search Warrant, Lieutenant Detective Patrick T. Sullivan, 2.

Mel Paunovich, from Southfield Police Department, was then asked to process the evidence. He was asked to because according to him, the medical examiner, Robert Sillery, was known to be sloppy concerning evidence. Sillery had allegedly been observed smoking a cigar and drinking alcohol during an early morning autopsy. This order allegedly came from Oakland County Assistant Prosecutor, Richard Thompson.

Medical Examiner Sillery autopsied the remains of other OCCK victims, and also suspect Christopher Busch.[120] Apparently the Oakland County Prosecutor had no problem with this.

In 1976 Paunovich was working as an evidence technician and running the Evidence Tech Bureau of Southfield Police Department. Paunovich told Detective Williams that he got a call that Mark Stebbins's body was found lying by a brick wall behind the New Orleans Strip Mall at 10 Mile Rd., and Greenfield Rd. in the city of Southfield. Paunovich then called the Oakland County Chief Assistant Prosecutor, Richard Thompson, who authorized Paunovich to move Mark Stebbin's body to the Southfield Police Department garage for processing instead of the medical examiner's office. Thompson had supposedly checked with the Oakland County Prosecutor, L. Brooks Patterson to get authorization for this.

Mel Paunovich told Detective Williams that he did in fact collect hairs, human and animal, from Mark Stebbins's clothing and turned the evidence over to Charlotte Day at the MSP Lab in Sterling Heights. Then he said he got a call from Charlotte Day approximately two to four weeks later informing him that they had

---

120 Supplementary Report, Ferndale Police Department, Detective Frank, February 19, 1976, 12:40 pm.

a bad flood in the basement of the lab and his evidence from Mark Stebbins was lost. So when Paunovich heard about the hairs matching those found on Mark Stebbins and Timothy King he remembered what Charlotte Day had told him and he wasn't clear on what hairs found on Mark Stebbins had come back a match to those of Timothy King.

Mel Paunovich discussed his theories with Detective Williams of who he thought was the OCCK. He said he always thought it was a police officer or a priest. Paunovich also stated that the OCCK could have been a cop because of his feeling that the suspect had a police radio.

Detective Williams then told Paunovich that Arch Sloan had a CB radio in his wreckers. Paunovich said that it was Ross Towing that towed for Southfield Police back then, and had one of their police prep radios right in their office at their tow yard. Williams said that he thought a witness in the past had mentioned Sloan driving for Ross Towing in the 70's or he had at least picked up and/or dropped off cars at the Ross Tow yard on Telegraph in Southfield.

Detective Williams then switched gears and asked Mel Paunovich to explain all the crime scenes he went to during the OCCK case and any evidence he may have handled other than that of Mark Stebbins. Paunovich said that he was at the Stebbins scene along with the Michelich scene and that was it. He went on to elaborate that he had nothing to do with the King case at all and the only evidence he handled on any of the cases was that of Mark Stebbins. Paunovich then stated that he never felt that the suspect that shot Jill Robinson was the same suspect that killed Mark Stebbins and Timothy King.

Detective Williams duly noted this in his observations.

Paunovich, being an evidence expert type of guy, thought that the suspect knew too much when or where the cops were or would be, and knew about trace evidence. Detective Williams then told Mel Paunovich that they were clearing everyone who had handled any evidence related to the OCCK with a DNA swab. He requested that Paunovich provide him with a DNA sample and explained that it was important regarding the integrity of the investigation. Paunovich said he would not consent to that, saying it was silly and said why didn't someone just call and ask him for a DNA sample? Detective Williams then showed the search warrant to Mel Paunovich that had been signed by Judge Timothy Kenny of the 3rd Circuit Court. Paunovich saw Judge Kenny's name and stated he knew the judge and that they were friends. He said the judge could have just called him and asked him for a DNA sample.

Detective Williams explained to Paunovich that it was his understanding that he had been approached in the past for a sample of his DNA by Lieutenant Kelly McCummell of Southfield Police Department. Paunovich said he had a falling out with Lieutenant McCummell and told her to go get a search warrant.

Detective Willams then buccal swabbed Mel Paunovich. Williams noted that the swabs were tagged, stored and turned over to the FBI Lab in Quantico, Virginia, for analysis.[121]

During the procurement of the body and the processing of the cooler that was confiscated from John Crosbie, there was quite a lot of evidence that was obtained pertaining to victim Mark Stebbins:

Fur and hair from the victim's jacket
Dirt from parking lot near body

---

[121] Wayne County Prosecutor's Office Grand Jury investigation, 196-8.

Dirt from under body
Dirt from around body
Rag from parking lot near body
Swabs from the cooler confiscated from Crosbie's Chevy
Hair from the cooler from suspect's car
Swabs from rear passenger top side of seat (white stains on the black vinyl seat cover)
Hair, fur and dirt from suspect's car
Hair, from the rear seat of suspect's car
Hair from the rear passenger floor
Victim's blue parka jacket with fur hood
Victim's Levi blue jeans with black belt
Suspect's blue knit jacket from rear deck
Victim's boots—bright blue paint and different color soils on boots
Victim's hair, pulled from various area of scalp at morgue
Red fibers from floor mats of suspects 65 Chevy
Red fibers taken from victim's Levis
Red mats from suspect's Chevy
Rope from trunk of suspect's car
Brick from rear driver's side floor of suspect's car
Blanket used to cover body
Victim's socks
Undershorts of victim
T-shirt of red sweatshirt of victim
The paper which was placed under the body by morgue transportation attendants

Dirt from the other side of brick wall from where the body was found[122]

Officer Frank was present with Corporal Paunovich when the above evidentiary items were processed.[123]

On December 6, 2010 Detective Williams received the Detroit Police file into the investigation of Arch Sloan on the two CSC 1st degree cases that Sloan committed in 1983 in Detroit and was subsequently arrested for in Farmington Hills in 1984. Williams noted that the file contained detailed important information about Sloan and included incident reports and pre-sentence reports on his arrests for CSC in 1970 in Pennsylvania for 6 counts of forced sodomy on boys. The file also contained the detailed family history of Arch Sloan, and psychiatric evaluations prior to sentencing in 1972, which were prior to the sentencing to two life sentences which he is currently serving.[124]

The file also revealed that Sloan was on the run for many months during the OCCK case and was possibly being aided by Detroit Police Sergeant Richard Clayton, who might have hid Sloan on his property in Montmorency County called "El Rancho farm."

The El Rancho farm was where Sloan had molested a victim in 1978 and was subsequently charged. Clayton was very evasive about Sloan and about his property in Montmorency County during an interview with Detroit Police. Victims described the farm as

---

[122] Narrative Report, Southfield Police Department, 11:50 am, February 19, 1976.
[123] Investigative Follow-up, Homicide, Mark Stebbins, Gerald Stonebraker, February 19, 1976.
[124] Wayne County Prosecutor's Office Grand Jury investigation, 7, 8.

having long rows of pine trees lining the driveway as you pulled in.[125]

Detective Williams met with Livonia Detectives on the OCCK case on December 15, 2010 to discuss the lead into Arch Sloan and John Crosbie. Williams also noted that the Livonia Police had pulled out of the Task Force once he retired and that Jessica Cooper, Oakland County Prosecutor, had convened her own grand jury to try to block Wayne County.[126]

On the morning of January 14, 2011, Detectives Williams, White and Matouk from the Wayne County Prosecutors office executed a search warrant at the home of Betty Roe (John Crosbie's sister). Detectives were searching for John Crosbie's belongings. After interviewing Betty Roe, and her son, Dante Roe, Detective Williams believed that Crosbie's personal property was located in his sister's home.[127]

Detectives began searching the northwest bedroom of the home that appeared to be used as a storage room, and began to find some old belongings of John Crosbie. Unable to locate the boxes that Dante had previously described to him, Detective Williams confronted Betty about possibly moving the boxes since being contacted by him the previous week. She said it was possible that Dante may have moved them to the garage.

Williams then observed a hatch in the ceiling of the closet in the northwest bedroom that led into the attic. He crawled up through the hatch into the attic area and found some items neatly stacked and face-up on top of the insulation near the opening: Two *Teen* movie magazines, a *Tiger Beat* magazine from 1977, and on

---

125 Ibid., 8,20.
126 Ibid., 8.
127 Ibid., 13.

top of that another *Teen* magazine covered in dust; with the date visible, December 1976.

Also lying near the magazines was a book, the *Wizard of Oz*. To the left of the book was a young woman or girl's blue knit button shirt with golden thread piping around the sleeves.

Detective Williams recovered these items from the crawl space attic and carefully placed them into paper envelopes. He then asked Betty about the items and she stated she didn't know anything was in the attic, nor did she know why these particular items would be there. She said she had a teenage daughter at the time of the OCCK, but didn't see why she would place those things in the attic. Williams then questioned Betty about her brother John coming to her home in Brighton to stay with her, which she replied he would come see her from time to time and sometimes bring their mother with him. She didn't remember him spending the night back in the 70's, but said it was possible.[128]

The Grand Jury testimony of Betty Roe was on January 19, 2011. Detective Williams had served Betty Roe a subpoena to appear in front of the Grand Jury and testify on this date. The subpoena also mandated that she produce any other personal belongings of her brother John that had been removed from her home or had not been recovered during the search warrant process.

Betty appeared carrying a small empty old gray suitcase that she thought had belonged to John, but did not know how he got it.

During the course of her testimony one of the things Betty talked about was that John was picked up by the Task Force for questioning concerning the disappearance of Mark Stebbins. She said she was living in Brighton, Michigan at the time, a single

---

128 Ibid.

parent raising four kids, when her mother called her about John's arrest. She told the Grand Jury that she came to Ferndale with her mother, and went to the Ferndale Police station where John was being held. She remembered going into a room to speak with John, who was behind some glass, but stated she couldn't recollect what they talked about. She was then asked when John was released the following day if they discussed why he was arrested by the Task Force in connection with the murder of Mark Stebbins. She stated that they never discussed it. Even though she had told detectives previously that she and John were very close and that he would often call her.

Detective Williams confronted Betty Roe with this obvious discrepancy, asking her how could it possibly be that she drove to Ferndale at the time John was being questioned; stayed at their family home, and yet never asked John what was going on? She stated that no, they didn't talk about what was going on.[129]

In an earlier interview Betty Roe had told Detective Williams that her and her family knew the Stebbins family, and that Ruth and Mark Stebbins would go to the Rialto Restaurant in Ferndale, where Betty's mom Edna worked. Betty also said that John Crosbie would also eat at this restaurant and that Mark Stebbins was possibly the Crosbie's paperboy in Ferndale.[34] She told Detective Williams that prior to and during the time of the child killings, John was hanging out at a lot of bars in Ferndale such as the Nu-Way, Stan's and the VFW.[130]

Betty Roe mentioned to Detective Williams that John Crosbie and Mark Stebbins's mother, Ruth, were friends before

---

129 Ibid., 14.
130 Ibid., 10.

they both passed away. Williams thought that was rather strange and duly noted this in the report.[131]

On October 22, 2014, Detectives William and MacArthur interviewed Arch Sloan at Gus Harrison Correctional Facility in Adrian, Michigan. This was Detective Williams first interview with Sloan. Detective Williams brushed up on his notes and compiled all the interview transcripts of Sloan and highlighted all the inconsistencies in his story throughout his past interviews.[132]

Williams noted that there had been many interviews of Sloan over the past four years, but that this would be the first confrontational interview.

Arch Sloan was unhappy when he entered the interview room and complained about missing his lunch for the interview. He then started complaining about missing his garden.

For approximately three hours the detectives went over the names of past associates and victims that he had failed to tell detectives about in the past. Detective Williams showed Arch Sloan the transcripts, and pointed out where he had been lying to detectives. Williams described how Sloan had selective memory, of how he could describe the inside of a car he worked on over twenty years ago, but didn't remember victims who all remembered him, or a tow yard at 8 Mile and Merriman back in the 70's that he towed cars to.

Detective Williams then started drilling down the inconsistencies in his stories. He confronted Sloan about the night Mark Stebbins's body was dumped at 10 Mile and Greenfield. Sloan had called the police from Macraken's gas station at 10 Mile

---

131 Ibid., 12.
132 Ibid.

and Middlebelt to say he would be there working late. Sloan said he had called in the past when he was working late. Williams was ready for this response. He said that was the *only* time time that Sloan had ever done that, and lo and behold a boy's body is dumped that night right down the road.

Arch Sloan stared at Detective Williams. He looked as if he had seen a ghost. Williams continued:

"You may have just loaded that kid on the floorboard of your wrecker and dumped him, that right Arch? 'Cause no one looks twice at a wrecker do they Arch, cops just wave as they go by at the wrecker drivers, right?

Detective MacArthur observed that Sloan's hands were shaking uncontrollably.

Detective Williams realized that after a grueling 2.5 to 3 hour interview Sloan just took it. He never once said he was hungry, or it was all bullshit or asked to leave.

Realizing Sloan was probably primed to perhaps cut a deal concerning the case, Detective Williams threw him a life line. He told him that it was possible to get out of prison, and to finally see the light of day before he died. Williams explained that this would be dependent on his culpability and cooperation that would confirm the facts of the case.

Detective Williams explained to Arch Sloan that his sentencing judge, Judge Talbot, would be the only person in the world who could make something like this a possibility, but it was entirely up to him.

After listening to what Williams had said, Sloan replied that if he were to give anyone a call it would be to Denise — referring to Lieutenant Denise Powell of the MSP.[133]

---

[133] Ibid., 151, 152.

Chapter 10

The Magical Mystery Tour

Detectives began investigating occult involvement in the OCCK very early on in the case. A mysterious man named Wayne Forest West appeared as a suspect in regards to various clues regarding the murders. He was under heavy surveillance and was also interviewed for his possible knowledge regarding the murders.

West was ex-communicated from Anton Lavey's Church of Satan.

He was thought to have an assumed identity. Wayne Forest West wasn't his real name. He had a limp, spoke with a British accent, and carried a walking stick.[134] His original church was called the Babylon Grotto in Birmingham, Michigan.[135] His second church was called the First Occultic Church of Man. In an article from *The Cloven Hoof* newsletter attributed to Anton Lavey, head of the Church of Satan in San Francisco, the church claimed to have a complete dossier on the man known as Wayne Forest West. They knew his real name, his past occupation, criminal record, condition

---

[134] Special Assignment, Timothy King Homicide, March 30, 1977, 8:00 am to 10:00 pm.

[135] Lee Winfrey, "Devil's Followers Increase," *Detroit Free Press*, April 13, 1971.

under which he had "traveled," sexual preoccupation and health record; everything before he had joined the Church of Satan.[136]

Mrs Anton Lavey was interviewed via phone by detectives in the Detroit Police Department. She was asked questions regarding Wayne Forest West. Detectives attempted to interview West at his apartment when he did not show up for a scheduled interview. He immediately called his sister and told her, "They're here." She was at his apartment within five minutes and told him not to talk to the police without an attorney present.[137] Under her own regard she had mentioned the OCCK investigation. She had also told the detectives they weren't going to get West's fingerprints.[138]

Detectives Bone and Turney then proceeded to interview West with his attorney present. When asked if he saw any similarity or ritualistic pattern in regards to the OCCK murders he said no. He also answered in the negative as to discerning a pattern when the children were taken or where their bodies were placed.[139]

The Wayne County Medical Examiner, Werner Spitz, suggested that detectives should contact Emmanuel Tanay, a psychiatrist in the area for a personality profile of the killer. Tanay was allowed to listen to the taped conversation that detectives had with Mrs Anton LaVey. He then excitedly stated that West could very well be the killer, and a was a very good suspect. The Oakland County Task force then gave all the information they had regarding

---

136 Hiley Ward, "One Grotto Becomes 'Occultic' Church: Satan Rift Centers in Detroit," *Detroit Free Press*, March 25, 1972.
137 Special Assignment, March 29, 1977 and April 6, 1977.
138 Special Assignment, March – April, 1977.
139 Interview: Mr Wayne West, Detectives Bone and Turney. Detroit Police Department, 3:00 pm, April 18, 1977.

Wayne Forest West to another psychiatrist, Dr Donald Rossi. He too felt that West was a very good suspect.[140]

The United States Immigration Service was then contacted to determine the real identity of Wayne Forest West. After an investigation it was found that West had given authorities false identification regarding his identity and he was arrested for supplying false information to a federal agent. Through the immigration investigator and the federal prosecutor, an arrangement was made for West that if he were to take a polygraph regarding the OCCK case all charges would be dropped in federal court. He refused. His case was scheduled in federal court and he was released on a personal bond of ten thousand dollars.

Sources then notified the investigators that West had left the state and would not be in court at the given date.[141]

West appeared to have distanced himself from the Church of Satan, but at one time held quite a bit of power within the organization. In 1971 he visited the Central Grotto of The Church of Satan in San Francisco to presumably to meet with head members, Anton Lavey and Michael Aquino. Aquino also sent West carbon copies of much of his correspondence. But then Diane Lavey, Anton Lavey's wife, communicated to Aquino her misgivings that West wanted to know more about what was going on in other Church of Satan grottos rather than being concerned with his own. Shortly after this communique of Diane Lavey to Michael Aquino, Wayne Forest West dissolved the Babylon

---

140 Special Assignment, March – April, 1977.
141 Ibid.

Grotto.[142] Aquino attributed the Babylon Grotto dissolution by West to a newsletter article by Anton Lavey disparaging aspiring Satanists from reading Aleister Crowley and Israel Regardie which supposedly angered West.[143] Yet West told Detroit detectives that he had scarcely heard of Crowley, and had never heard of Regardie, even though he was a high priest in The Church of Satan.[144] He had also stated the same in a Detroit Free Press article that "...the "Satanic Bible" is swiped from a number of occult books, among them "The Confessions of Aleister Crowley, of [which] LaVey has banned his followers from reading."[145]

West's colleague in the Church of Satan, Michael Aquino, was a Lieutenant Colonel in Military Intelligence in the U.S. Army, and along with other various military specialties listed on his resume, he had also received numerous awards.[146] Aquino had been implicated in child abuse and mind control programming by many victims. Psychological professionals learned from victims about a mind control programming termed "Monarch." They said that the government/military and cooperating Satanic and/or pagan cults were responsible for implementing the atrocities perpetrated on these victims. These cults are often multi-generational, and their parents donate their own children to be programmed with drugs and electric shock. Other children are kidnapped and sold into this

---

142 Michael Aquino, The Church of Satan, 5th ed., (San Francisco, 2002) 139-41.
143 Aquino, *Church of Satan*, 135.
144 Interview Wayne West, Bone and Turney, 13.
145 Hiley Ward, "Satan Rift."
146 Aquino, *Church of Satan*, 986.

programming situation or are brought into it gradually through various day-cares.

Paul Bonacci, a victim of the Franklin Scandal, along with many other child victims, went into great depth about the central role of Michael Aquino in this depravity.[147] According to Noreen Gosch, her son Johnny Gosch was kidnapped in 1982 and paid for by Michael Aquino weeks after he was kidnapped. Aquino was referred to as the "Colonel" and investigative reports have connected him not only to the kidnapping of Johnny Gosch, but also to cases involving Eugene Martin, Jacob Wetterling and other Midwestern boys.[148] According to Paul Bonacci, who added in the kidnap of Johnny Gosch, Johnny was repeatedly raped and molested while being photographed for pornography before being taken by Aquino to Colorado.[149]

During the time period that the children from the OCCK case were being abducted, held and then murdered, a number of items were stolen from Catholic churches in Detroit and the surrounding areas. The recorded day these items began to vanish, on February 14, 1976, was the day before Mark Stebbins was abducted. The items included candle holders, church vestments, clerical clothing, six stations of the cross, chalices, and cases of candles.[150] According to the Missa Solemnis (The Black Mass) written as an abomination of the Roman Catholic Mass by Wayne

---

147 John W. DeCamp, *The Franklin Cover-Up: Child Abuse, Satanism, and Murder in Nebraska*, 2nd ed., (Lincoln: AWT Inc., 1996), 328.
148 Noreen N. Gosch, *Why Johnny Can't Come Home*, (West Des Moines: The Johnny Gosch Foundation, 2000), 223.
149 Gosch, Johnny Can't Come Home, 247.
150 Special Assignment, 118.

Forest West for the Church of Satan, consecrated items must be obtained from the Roman Catholic Church to perform this ritual.[151]

Kathleen Sorenson, a foster mother who took care of children who had been through satanic ritual abuse, stated that there were particular things that were common in children's stories when they talked about devil worship, "There are things that come up in every single story, such as candles. They all talk about sex. Sex is without a doubt a part of every area of this, all sorts of perverted sex."

The children were also blackmailed into silence by their abusers by the threat of showing the police the pornography that they were involved in.[152]

West was described as aristocratic, temperamental, artistic, a Shakespearean actor-type, highly intelligent, with the ability to converse at length on many subjects.[153]

Perhaps like Aleister Crowley, Wayne Forest West was an occulted secret agent 666.[154] It was most likely that Wayne Forest West was tapping into the occult network that Crowley had established in the U. S. many years earlier. Around 1918 Crowley had come to Detroit and set up an esoteric society called the Ordo Templi Orientis (OTO).[155] A meeting took place on April 13, 1919 at the Detroit Athletic Club in order to cement the foundations of

---

[151] Aquino, *Church of Satan*, 459.
[152] Gosch, *Johnny Can't Come Home*, 225.
[153] Special Assignment, 2-3.
[154] Richard B. Spence, *Secret Agent 666: Aleister Crowley, British Intelligence and the Occult*, (Port Townsend: Feral House, 2008), 6.
[155] William T. Noble, "Black Magic Once Detroit Cult Lives Ruined Decades Ago by Sorcerer Aleister Crowley." *Detroit News*, January 26, 1958.

the newly formed club. Prominent Detroit Freemasons signed pledges stating they had joined the order. US District Attorney Frank Murphy described the founding OTO members as "...big men." And where the mere "...mention of their names would bring on a scandal."[156]

At this point in time Crowley was working to unite Freemasonry under the OTO, as he thought it contained the true secrets of Freemasonry.[157] He also thought it had a definite connection with the New Aeon.[158] Others didn't feel so positive and felt that it was an occult order based on power, hypnotism, and black magic. Critics felt that because the ceremonies of the order were hypnotic, it created the necessary mental and astral atmosphere which hypnotized and prepared the members to be willing tools in the hands of the controlling adepts within the order.[159] There are also those who believe that the OTO is the probable command center of Satanism.[160]

According to the sources of Reina Michaelson, an Australian psychologist who received an award for her work on the prevention of sexual abuse regarding minors, the OTO is a

---

156 Richard Kaczynski, Panic in Detroit, (New York: Sekhmet Books, 2015), 19.
157 Kaczynski, *Panic*, 1.
158 Ibid., 42.
159 Nesta H. Webster, *Secret Societies and Subversive Movements*, (London: Boswell Printing and Publishing Co., LTD., 1924), 324.
160 Mark Burdman, "Satanists escalate war against Western civilization." *Executive Intelligence Review* 16, no. 1 (1989): 64.

paedophile ring, and some of its members practice trauma-based mind control as well as ritual abuse involving sex magic.[161]

In 1918 Crowley also began the Alamantrah working. This was a magickal working designed to open a doorway to the astral realm and contact various entities who resided within that dimension.[162] The Alamantrah working took place in Montauk, New York on Long Island between January 14 and June 16. This working was around the same time he was dealing with the Freemasons in Detroit in setting up the OTO.

Previous to this Detroit trip Crowley had visited the city back in 1915 to obtain refined peyote from the Parke-Davis pharmaceutical company. He used this drug in rituals, such as in *The Rites of Eleusis*.[163] *The Rites of Eleusis* were performed in London in October and November of 1910. They were performed as a series of seven one-act plays designed to create within the audience an altered state of consciousness.[164] Crowley clearly had established a business relationship with Parke-Davis Pharmaceuticals. He said that, "They were kind enough to interest themselves in my researches of *Anhalonium lewinii* [peyote] and made me some special preparations on the lines indicated by my

---

161 Alexandre LeBreton, *MK ULTRA, Ritual Abuse and Mind Control: Tools of Domination for the Nameless Religion*, (Ireland: Omnia Veritas Limited, 2021), 103, 104.
162 Spence, *Secret Agent 666*, 149.
163 Walter Bosley and Richard B. Spence, *Empire of the Wheel: Espionage, Murder and the Occult in Southern California*, (California: Corvos Books, 2011, Kindle Edition), Loc 2933.
164 Tracy W. Tupman, "Theatre Magick: Aleister Crowley and the Rites of Eleusis." (Dissertation, Ohio State University, 2003), 1.

experience which proved greatly superior to previous preparations."¹⁶⁵

Back in England Crowley's travels and machinations were closely watched and scrutinized by those suspicious of his motives. Private Detective George Makgill, who had his own detective agency, Section D, for the British Empire Union and the Economic League, was one of those who closely watched Crowley. Makgill had devoted a considerable amount of time to unmasking that cult of evil, and Aleister Crowley was the most definite spider in the center of that web of intrigue. He also linked Crowley to "international traffic in drugs and the traffic in women and children." ¹⁶⁶

It appeared that Crowley, aka The Beast, was the precursor for laying the foundations for the modern-day MK Ultra programs (mind control) by developing occult networks and finding initiates and devotees willing to carry on the cultic system.

---

165 Kaczynski, *Panic*, 21.
166 Spence, *Secret Agent 666*, 190.

Chapter 11

The Mysterious John McKinney

The mysterious death of John McKinney, Birmingham art gallery owner and minister happened around the time of the OCCK. Cops were quick to point out that the cases were not connected. Why they would utter this was a mystery unto itself and the more inquisitive minded mulled it over. There were few facts regarding the case that were published and it seemed there was a self-contained bubble being drawn around the murder.

It was much later that many people realized that John McKinney and his art connections most likely played a pivotal part in the OCCK case. Certain people, places and motivations made this realization possible.

And John McKinney was a mysterious character. He was involved in a series of enigmatic relationships that were puzzling to the police. Some people thought he was gay. Some people did not. Some people thought he was having an affair with one woman. Some people did not. Some people thought he was having an affair with another woman. Some people did not. And on it went. One thing people could agree upon was that he was estranged from his wife.

According to a police report dated September 20 1977, the Birmingham Police Department received a routine call from the

Fire Department for assistance with first-aid at the Birmingham Art Gallery, located at 1025 Haynes Street. When the officers arrived at the scene they found gallery owner, John McKinney, dead on the floor. He had an injury to the back of his head which resulted in massive bleeding. The officers noted there was no apparent evidence of a robbery. It was established that employee, Steve Accomando, had discovered the body. The MSP Crime Laboratory was called to examine the scene.[167]

A call came in early afternoon of that day from a tipster who preferred to remain anonymous. He told the officer that he should check out a Dr Harry Phillips. He said he had heard John McKinney talking to Mrs Phillips, and that Dr Harry Phillips was getting a divorce from his wife. He thought that there was some sort of triangle involved.[168]

After the initial observation of the body of John McKinney, detectives were then tasked with figuring out what had actually happened prior to the murder. The police photographer described the body lying face up in a pool of blood just a short distance from the small entrance door adjacent to the parking lot. McKinney was clothed in a blue jeans jacket and pants that someone would later remark seemed too young of apparel for his age. There were blood smears and drippings all around the body that led to a first-floor bathroom. The blood drippings also led upstairs.[169]

The MSP crime lab photographed the body and obtained blood samples from the various locations around the gallery and dusted for fingerprints.

---

[167] City of Birmingham Police Department, Narrative Report, Homicide, Officer L. Solomon, 10:10 am, September 27, 1977.
[168] Telephone Conversation, Sergeant Mohr, 2104 Hours, September 20, 1977.
[169] Birmingham, Officer Solomon.

It appeared to the investigators that the original incident concerning John McKinney occurred upstairs in his office on the second floor. It also appeared as if some sort of blunt instrument was used to whack McKinney on the head. This then caused blood to spill over to wall paneling and the window in the office. Then it looked as if McKinney had struggled to get down the stairs. There was a blood trail leading out of the office and down the steps to the first-floor bathroom where was a considerable amount of blood in the sink.

The autopsy was performed by Dr Robert J. Sillery, MD. This was the same doctor that had performed autopsies on three of the victims of the OCCK.

Dr Sillery discovered bruises and cuts on the victim's lower arm areas and back, indicating he had been involved in a struggle. He had sustained a broken nose and black and blue bruises to his scrotum. The death of John McKinney was caused by a bullet to the left temple.

In the bathroom on the lower-level MSP technicians had confiscated a piece of rope as evidence which was lying on the floor.[170]

Detectives began to dig into McKinney's relationships and business dealings. According to Cary Wilkie, a friend and employee in McKinney's gallery, John was considering a divorce for several years. Wilkie said he had a girlfriend named Linda Webster and that

---

[170] City of Birmingham Police Department, Narrative Report: Follow-up Investigation, Homicide, Officer L. Solomon, 10:10 am, September 21, 1977, 1-3.

McKinney's business had been very bad. He didn't think he was a homosexual though, or was involved with narcotics.[171]

McKinney was an ordained minister and taught Sunday school. He ministered to people at the Bloomfield Nursing Home. His friend in pastoral activities was Ida Jennings and she knew about the girlfriend, Linda Webster. Ida Jennings said she knew John McKinney very well. She said that John was going to break it off with Linda since he had been getting more involved in church and being called more of God. And because of that he knew he couldn't get a divorce because it was not in the way of God. There was that, and then there was this other thing.

Ida Jennings said that about three weeks ago that John was quite disturbed about something. They began to talk about it and he told her that he was going to have to do something about a man who worked for him. Then a few days later he said he would have to let him go because of some things. He didn't say what things though. Ida Jennings said John McKinney loved the Lord and wouldn't touch narcotics or any other intoxicants. She vehemently denied that John was a homosexual.[172]

John McKinney's son, John Mark McKinney, knew Linda Webster was his father's girlfriend. He did not have a problem with his father's lifestyle. Gallery employee, Steve Accomando, was dating his sister, but he only knew a little bit about Steve and didn't even know that Steve had quit the gallery for some time.

---

[171] City of Birmingham Police Department, Detective Bureau, Det. Richard Chambers, Homicide, 3:17 pm, September 20, 1977.
[172] City of Birmingham Police Department, Detective Bureau, Det. Richard Chambers and Officer Larry Solomon, Homicide, 3:58 pm, September 21, 1977.

John explained that he and Doug and Linda Webster used to go to a lot of places. And that Doug was a partner with his dad at the gallery. Doug Webster now lived in Arizona. John felt that his father could have had homosexual tendencies.

Detectives told John that whoever was in his father's office the night he was murdered was drinking wine. John said his father would not allow a lot of people in his office unless it was an important matter or they were personal friends.

"Who do you think your father would allow up there to drink wine with?" asked detectives.

"Cary, Doug, Linda and another [redacted] person." replied John.

During the night of John McKinney's murder, up in the office, there was some hash pipe smoking going on. John said he knew that his dad smoked marijuana, but did not know if the hash pipe was his or not.

John was asked about Shirley Essex Phillips, the wife of Dr Harry Phillips, who was mentioned by the anonymous tipster, and John said yes, he had heard of her at the gallery. John told detectives that he thought it was possible that Cary Wilkie, a once long-time employee, could have had a falling out with his father.[173]

Mr George Landino had some information for Birmingham detectives. He said he worked in the Little Barium School System and that he worked with John McKinney for about three years and knew him for approximately twenty years. He felt he had some keen insight into the workings of his personality. He said that he thought

---

173 Information Statement, Sergeant Malcolm Mohr, Officer Larry Solomon, Interview of Mark McKinney, son of victim.

that McKinney was a determined individual, a fine person, and a good worker that worked long, hard hours. He seemed very calm and intellectual and would give you good advice. Not only that, but he had a bit of a temper regarding clients, especially when he wasn't paid on time.

The last time Landino had seen John McKinney was at the Cranbrook art auction. He said he knew that things with his wife, Yvonne McKinney, were not smooth and that Yvonne McKinney seemed to use Mrs Landino as a sounding board to talk about her problems.[174]

The medical examiner, Doctor Sillery, couldn't determine the approximate time of death. He stated that there was no accurate way of determining time of death. And elaborated that the only way you could validate time of death was when he [John McKinney] was last seen alive and when he was first seen deceased. So it would be between these two points.

Sillery went on to wonder if there was a safe in the gallery, and that maybe the killer(s) wanted McKinney to open up the safe and he didn't want to. Sergeant Mohr told him the safe was always open.

"Well it may not have money per se," Sillery replied, "but it may have been some art object that they wanted and he wouldn't tell them where it was."

"It's possible." said Sergeant Mohr, "However, he's careful about who he lets in his building and from all indications, it's his

---

[174] Birmingham Police Department, Detective Bureau, Homicide of John McKinney, Det. Richard Chambers, 3:07 pm, September 21, 1977.

friends, somebody he trusts enough to come up and give him wine, etc."

Sergeant Mohr then went on to discuss the procured evidence found in the downstairs bathroom — a cord. The cord was red and yellow and vertically stripped. It was the kind you would find on a drape sash or Venetian blind, and it was approximately four and a half feet long. He wondered if it was used to tie up John McKinney.

Sillery didn't think so. There was no evidence of binding marks. He felt someone was holding him when he received the vicious beating.[175]

Detectives went to speak with Cary Wilkie again, and advised him of his rights via Miranda warning. Wilkie agreed to answer their questions without the presence of an attorney.

He was asked if he was a detective investigating the homicide who he would investigate first, or who would he check as possible suspects. Wilkie stated that he would investigate Shirley Essex's husband, and Ronald Frey.

Ronald Frey was an artist who used to work for McKinney.

Detectives asked if Linda Webster loved John.

"Oh yes." said Cary Wilkie.

Detectives then asked if he had ever met Dr Phillips. Wilkie said Dr Phillip's wife had an emotional relationship with John and that it was not physical. He said that Dr Phillips was madly and insanely in love with his wife and that he considered John a threat.

---

[175] Tape recorded conversation between Dr Sillery and Sergeant Malcolm Mohr.

He said that he had heard that John was supposedly having an affair with Shirley Essex Phillips.

Wilkie felt that it was unlikely that John had any homosexual tendencies. And that John was not Linda Webster's boyfriend.

Apparently Steve Accomando had related to Wilkie once that a certain person was a partner in the gallery and that this person was very wealthy and fronted a lot of the financial backing for the work at the gallery. And this person was not a talented artist.

Detectives asked Wilkie about the type of key holder McKinney had for his car keys. He said it was a circular type of key holder with a British flag insignia on the emblem and they were in a black case.

John had taken a trip with a [redacted] person of interest to London, England.

At the close of the interview Cary Wilkie said that detectives should interview Bob Garelick, who owned an art gallery in Arizona. He said John did not like, nor trust Garelick. Neither one of them had anything nice to say about each other.[176]

Investigators then began to drill down on what was the exact nature of McKinney's dubious "love" triangle dealings. Birmingham detectives, Sargeant Malcolm Mohr and Officer Larry Solomon visited with a Mr Patten, who did work for the gallery. He too was asked the question of where he would begin this homicide investigation, and replied with Linda Webster, Shirley Essex Phillips or her husband.

---

176 Sergeant Malcolm Mohr, Officer Larry Solomon, Interview of Cary Wilkie, 3:05 pm, September 22, 1977.

He was then asked if John was acting as a mediator in a possible love triangle. He stated he did not know. But said that Shirley and Linda both knew each other. When questioned if McKinney could possibly be bisexual he said that several years ago at a party he had made advances to his brother-in-law.

Mr Patten did the certified public accounting (CPA) work for McKinney's gallery. He was asked if John was well-off and if someone could profit from the murder. He said that the first of September this year sales were up by twenty percent and bills payable were down to $15,000 from $26,000. He said McKinney had a valuable art collection in the gallery that was worth around $500,000.[177]

During the formal statement from Steve Accomando, employee of John McKinney's Birmingham Gallery, where he was fingerprinted and palm printed for the process of elimination, he stated that after the murder a gold chair in the gallery was out of place. The gold chair was sitting outside the downstairs bathroom with its back up against the wall. There wasn't any blood on the chair, but there was a quantity of blood on the door jamb that could have been brushed there by the back of someone's head while sitting in the chair. Steve also admitted that he knew McKinney had a girlfriend by the name of Linda and that last week she was at the gallery and McKinney had spoken her name. When she left Accomando asked, "Is that the

---

177 Information Statement, Sergeant Malcolm Mohr, Officer Larry Solomon, Interview of Michael Patten, CPA to victim, 2:40 pm, September 22, 1977.

Linda that I'm not supposed to discuss or mention around the house?"[178] McKinney said yes.

After interviewing Accomando, detectives interviewed Yvonne McKinney, the wife of John McKinney. She described the key case of her husband. The officers involved in the investigation had been unable to find the keys.[179]

On September 20, 1977, Detectives Marble and Winkelman of the Birmingham Police Department, were working tips on the OCCK case for the Oakland County Task Force. After their lunch they were notified to respond to the homicide scene at the Birmingham Gallery. After viewing the body and contacting Mr Kleine concerning the Detroit Art Dealers Association meeting that John McKinney was supposed to attend but didn't, they left to interview Linda Webster.

Linda said she had last seen John McKinney at a coffee shop where they had dinner on September 18, 1977. She said she was waiting for a friend from the Banner Linen Company. She stated that she knew a [redacted] particular subject when she was a little girl and her ex-husband, Doug Webster, was part owner of the Birmingham Gallery and was beneficiary or executor of the gallery, but he left a year ago in June. He had addresses in Arizona and California.

---

178 Birmingham Police Department, Detective Bureau, Homicide of John McKinney, Interview of Steve Accomando, Det. Richard Chambers, 10:04 am, September 22, 1977.
179 Birmingham Police Dept., Detective Bureau.

She said she had divorced Doug Webster in May of 1976 and that John's wife Yvonne was aware of her for around four years. She said she had no hassle from Yvonne.

Linda stated that John's concerns were with the gallery, church, mental health, teen-age problems, and he was on the board of BlueCross-BlueShield. McKinney also had other connections with psychiatrists in the area in regards to counseling.

She stated that the only problem that she knew of at this point in time in McKinney's life was that he was involved in the counseling of Harry and Shirley Essex, who was an artist in the gallery. This counseling involved a triangle affair with a boyfriend of Shirley Essex named Bowen Brock of Brock Reality. McKinney was trying to reconcile their marriage.[180]

Detectives then went to talk to Linda Webster's friend who worked at the Banner Linen Company, which was owned by his parents. He stated that he and John McKinney were best friends and that he had known him since 1971. They had went to London together in September of 1976 and had become even closer friends.

Detectives then turned to Shirley Essex Phillips. On September 20, 1977, they paid her a visit. Mrs Phillips stated that she did know John McKinney and that they were preparing a show at the gallery in December. She said she had known McKinney for about twenty years. As an alibi she stated that she was home on Sunday night and she was with her husband in the morning on Monday. Then she

---

[180] Birmingham Police Department, Narrative Report, Homicide of John McKinney, Detectives Winkelman and Marble, September 22, 1977.

went to the Sommerset Mall, ate dinner at Capachina's in the mall, and left, then did some further shopping in Holly.

Detectives asked about the alleged boyfriend, Mr Brock. She said she did see him on Monday from about 5:30 to 6:00, and had known him for approximately twenty years. She said he was a client of hers and she was painting a portrait of Mr Brock's father, who was dying.

Detectives knew she was lying at this point in time. She did not elaborate on her relationship with Brock or say she had spent the day with Brock. Or divulge any information in regards to her husband being involved in a fight or the counseling with John McKinney.

Shirley Essex Phillips stated her husband was Dr Henry H. Phillips who was an optometrist at the Fenton Medical Center. This was her second marriage. Her first husband was deceased, and his last name was Santo. Her husband did own a [redacted] type of car that the investigators were looking into. Her father, Joe Essex, was a retired Ferndale police officer.

Shirley Essex Phillips did mention she did know Linda Webster, John's girlfriend, and she knew of problems with her marriage. But she had never met her. She knew of Doug Webster and that McKinney had received a call from him approximately one month ago and had asked him to come out to Arizona to see him. She also knew of Sally Saunders, owner of tennis courts and investor in the Birmingham Gallery. She said another person that McKinney worked for was Peggy LaSalle, who was from the Little Gallery in Birmingham.

Detectives described Shirley Essex Phillips as a very good looking woman.

Mrs Phillips knew that John and Linda Webster had gone to New York together and that Linda had wanted John McKinney to get a divorce from his wife. And there was tension in their relationship because he did not get a divorce from his wife.

She also knew that a man named John Blanchard and McKinney had gone to London together and that McKinney was supposed to come to her home in regards to a portrait of Judge Roth that she was painting for a show.

Detectives then contacted her husband, Mr Phillips, and asked him to return home to talk to them. He had been at a board meeting for the First National Bank of Fenton, of which he was head of the board. He had also been in the US Air Force as a navigator.

Mr Phillips stated that his alibi for the weekend was that Sunday he was home with his wife and son Chris, did some work around the house, and had a conversation with his next door neighbor approximately four times during the course of the day. Then he met with Mr Judd, one of the members of the bank and they had a business meeting from 5:30 until 7:00. They also had their eldest son home from college on Sunday. On Monday he was in the office from 8:00 am to 6:00 pm and that he had a full roster of appointments and one cancellation.

Detectives then turned again to Mrs Phillips. They informed her that they had information in regards to a fight that occurred in a cabin up north, in which her husband entered the cabin and struck her lover, Brock. She admitted to being at the cabin with Brock, and that she and her husband had been separated because of marital problems, and that John McKinney was counseling them. She said she had known and loved John McKinney for many years, but not physically.

Shirley Essex Phillips said that she and Brock had gotten a room under the name of Brock and Greenwald, at the Somerset Inn, on Monday, September 19, and they stayed in the room from approximately 2:50 until 7:00 pm. They had sex and then lunch. At around 7:00 pm they went back to her car and sat and talked. She left the Somerset Motel at approximately 8:00 pm and returned home.

She told detectives she was sorry that she had lied.

Detectives Marble and Winkelman went back to the station and discovered that a woman named Audrey, a waitress at the IHOP, said that a Mrs Yankee was at the IHOP at approximately 9:00 pm on September 19, 1977 and made statements to the effect of "Did you hear the owner of the Birmingham Gallery was killed?" Detectives contacted Audrey Cardinas, the waitress at the IHOP, and she confirmed that at 9:00 pm on September 19, 1977, thirteen hours before the body of John McKinney was reported to the Birmingham Police Department, that Mrs Gay Yankee was in the IHOP referring to a homicide at the gallery.

Then detectives took a call at 11:55 pm from Linda Webster who stated that she had received an anonymous phone call from a young female who stated that if she knew or was involved in the murder of John McKinney that she was going to kill her. Suggestions were then made to Linda Webster that she could go to the Birmingham Motel for protective custody or she could go to the Oakland County Jail for equal measures. She said she would have a friend stay with her overnight. Detectives then contacted Officer Baker, who was assigned to stay there overnight.

Detective then contacted Mrs Gay Yankee who confirmed that she was at the IHOP at approximately 9:00 pm on the nineteenth and stated she was referring to another homicide. This homicide was at the Art and Gems Gallery on Telegraph Rd and Irene, the manager, was shot and killed. This homicide occurred in the Pontiac/Waterford area.

Detectives had a discussion concerning the case and everyone was brought up to date regarding the homicide. An interview was made with Bowen Brock, boyfriend of Shirley Essex Phillips. Bowen Brock, owner of Brock Realty, was contacted by Detective Marble and appeared at Birmingham Police Station for an interview at 10:08 am. Brock had been in the US Air Force, airman 2nd class, a veteran who had received an honorable discharge. He had been in realty and real estate companies all of his life and was now owner of Brock Realty. His alibi for Monday, September 19th, was that he woke up at 9:00 am and went to his home office and was involved in a sale from 9:00 to 10:45 where he was closing the sale of a lot. He also worked on a title policy. Then around 10:45 he left and went to the Detroit Bank and Trust and was there until shortly after 11:00 am. At approximately 11:30 he arrived at the Somerset Inn where he made reservations under the name of Brock and Greenwald, where he was meeting Shirley Essex Phillips. He had a meeting at 12:00 noon at a restaurant on Orchard Lake called the Meeting Place. He went to lunch with the managers of the Orchard Lake and Waterford realty companies, introducing a new officer of the company. Then from 1:00 to 1:45 pm he was in the West Bloomfield office and from 1:45 to 2:30 he met with a client in regards to a real estate transaction. He was supposed to meet with Shirley Essex Phillips at the Somerset Inn at approximately 2:30

but did not arrive there until approximately 3:00 pm. From 3:00 until 7:00 pm he was with Shirley Brock in Room 229. The information had yet to be verified by detectives.

Bowen Brock stated that he no problems with John McKinney and that he had to talk to him via the counseling arrangements of himself, Shirley Essex Phillips and her husband Henry Phillips. He thought Mr Phillips was capable of harming him, and at one time had in fact taken a swing at him. But he did not believe he would do any harm to John McKinney.

Detectives mulled this over, went to lunch and returned to interview Mrs McKinney. They discovered that Detective Chambers had interviewed her prior to this. Detectives Marble and Winkelman asked her what items she remembered being in McKinney's office. She could remember two blue Ming lamps, with light beige silk lamp shades, two very old candlesticks, seven or eight different sized Buddhas, various taxidermy animal mounts, a brass set of wine cups, small ivory statuettes, a Japanese print in the bathroom; a small Rembrandt portrait and Oriental wall hangings.

She said that a [redacted] particular person had loaned money to John and that another [redacted] suspect had a beard. This was the alleged subject that had met McKinney at the Whistle Stop Restaurant. They also discussed the missing keys. One set of gallery keys were found in the vehicle by Detective Marble and returned to Mrs McKinney. Other gallery keys were located in the car, but these were not the same ones that John McKinney used. And the car keys were still missing.

Detectives then discovered that Linda Webster was at one time Linda Bender. Bender being apparently her maiden name. Her father was Bob Bender who owned B&W Controller. She said she has driven John's car on occasion, but didn't have keys to the car or the gallery. She said she talked to her husband, Doug on September 21, 1977 in Arizona. He lives in Scottsdale, Arizona and works at Yares Gallery. He also spent some time in La Jolla, California. She stated that the relationship between Doug and John McKinney was completely severed. John had bought Doug out, and that Doug had no longer had any connection to the gallery.

Detectives questioned Linda Webster in regards to a person of interest. She stated that she had known him since October of 1975 and that this [redacted] suspect never had a beard as long as she knew him.

They also questioned her in regards to a visitor she had on Monday night from approximately 8:00 pm to 11:00 pm. She said that this person was Kirk Falvey, an attorney in Ortonville. Then they asked her about her trip to New York, which she said was a Mary Beards opening and that Mary Beards is affiliated with Cranbrook. She said she went to New York with John McKinney but that John Blanchard did not go with them. They had left Friday of Labor Day weekend and had a good time. They returned to Michigan Sunday night.

She said she had been with John McKinney on two trips to New York and on two trips to Georgia. Linda mentioned that she and John had made an extended trip all throughout Kentucky. He had showed Linda where he had lived as a boy and where he was raised in Kentucky.

Detectives went to see a man who was known to John McKinney. They asked him about John McKinney ever having a friend with a beard. He said there was a guy named Cliff McChesney, who lived in the Williamston area. He said Ron Frey had a beard, and had shaved it within the last month.

He said John McKinney had made statements to him that he should go out with Linda Webster. He also made statements questioning how could he be in love with two women at the same time, Linda and Shirley.[181]

Then there was the interesting case of Michael Beatty, a relative of John McKinney. Michael Beatty became a suspect in the murder of John McKinney, and on Monday, October 9, 1978, Officer Mohr went over to talk with him. Michael Beatty did not want to take a polygraph test, but eventually wound up taking one. Officer Mohr then conferred with his father, Mr Beatty, who said he would contact law enforcement when he came to Michigan from Florida.

On Thursday, October 12, 1978, Mr Beatty came to the Birmingham Police Department and had written statements from people in Diamond City, Arkansas, stating that Michael Beatty was in fact in Diamond City at the time of the homicide. Officer Mohr placed a lot of weight on the statement of one Mrs Simpson. He had conferred with her by phone previously and she related that Michael Beatty had been in Arkansas at least two or three weeks prior to the homicide. He had stayed with them for the period of time running into October, and at no time did he leave town, he was present in Diamond City, Arkansas the whole time. Apparently Officer Mohr at first disbelieved this statement made by Mrs Simpson because Micheal Beatty had previously stated that he was in Michigan just a week prior to John McKinney's death.

---

181 Birmingham Police Department, Narrative Report, Sergeant Mohr, October 19, 1977.

It seemed Michael Beatty had an odd conception of time. He thought he talked to detectives a year ago, when in fact it was only a week ago. Officer Mohr assumed that since his conception of time was so off, he really did not know when he was in Michigan prior to John McKinney's death. So he took Mrs Simpson's word for it.

With this information Officer Mohr conferred with Sergeant Hanson, who had administered the polygraph for Michael Beatty. Michael Beatty had failed the test. He said that apparently Michael Beatty did have a valid alibi in Diamond City, Arkansas, and maybe the reason he failed the test was due to the fact that he feels he is possessed by Satan and that Satan killed John McKinney. And because of that maybe he felt somewhat responsible. Officer Mohr concluded that Michael Beatty was not responsible for killing John McKinney.[182]

Officer Mohr then met with Terry Watson, an old friend of Michael Beatty. He said he had known Michael Beatty since kindergarten and that Terry Watson's parents and Michael Beatty's parents were extremely close. He said that Michael Beatty had an extremely bad temper, he was always getting in fights, and Mr Watson was very careful what he said to him because he did not want to upset him because he would become extremely violent. But at no time had he ever attempted to harm Terry Watson.

Watson stated that Beatty carried a .22 caliber rifle in the rear of his pickup truck. And he was sure he was in the area when John McKinney was killed.

---

[182] Birmingham Police Department, Narrative Report, Follow-up Investigation, Sergeant Mohr, September 20, 1978.

On September 16, 1978, MSP officer from the Pontiac office went to the Watson's home looking for Michael Beatty. They said that a pickup truck belonging to Michael Beatty was found in Saint Ignace, Michigan at the Intersection of I-75 and US-2. The vehicle was impounded at Fred's Standard Station.[183]

On September 19, 1978 Officer Mohr received a phone call from the MSP in Saint Ignace. They stated they had found Michael Beatty, and that he was staying at the Traveler's Hotel in Saint Ignace. Officer Mohr said he would be coming up from Birmingham, Michigan and for them to keep an eye on Beatty until he arrived.

When Officer Mohr arrived, he told Micheal Beatty that he was under investigation for the homicide of John McKinney and was read his Miranda rights. Michael Beatty referred to John McKinney as Uncle Bill, being the adopted son of John McKinney's sister.

Beatty stated he had no idea who killed John McKinney and said he was in Arkansas at the time the homicide took place. Officer Mohr found it hard to get a specific answer from Michael Beatty, he was very evasive. He felt he had mental issues. Michael Beatty told him he was possessed by Satan and that it was his opinion that Satan was the one who killed his Uncle Bill. He also said that Satan made him do strange things. But he denied he had anything to do with John McKinney's homicide.

Michael Beatty was asked if he would return to Birmingham, Michigan with Officer Mohr to take a polygraph and he said he would. During the polygraph exam Beatty was asked if

---

[183] Birmingham Police Department, Narrative Report, Follow-up Investigation, Sergeant Mohr, October 9, 1978.

he killed his Uncle Bill. He replied in the negative. However, Sergeant Hanson, administrator of the polygraph, felt he was being deceptive, so he ran another set of tests. During this test Beatty was asked if Satan made him kill his Uncle Bill. Sergeant Hanson got a tremendous response on the polygraph in regards to this question. He felt that Michael Beatty was being deceptive in answering the examination questions and there was a strong possibility that he did in fact kill John McKinney. But although Sergeant Hanson extensively interviewed Michael Beatty, he was unable to get him to state that he in fact did kill John McKinney. Michael Beatty believed that Satan killed his Uncle Bill and that he was possessed by Satan. However, Satan did not make him kill Uncle Bill.

Officer Mohr said that if he felt he was possessed by Satan, he was just further playing into Satan's hand by lying about the killing of his Uncle Bill. That if in fact Satan made him kill Uncle Bill the only way he could purge his soul of Satan was by being truthful to Officer Mohr and admitting that he did kill his Uncle Bill. At this suggestion Beatty became extremely upset and began to perspire and shake. After a few minutes of not saying anything, he finally blurted out that he didn't do it.

The only way the officers could get any positive response from Michael Beatty was stating that only God could save him from Satan. And that God could not save him from Satan as long as he continued to play into Satan's hands by lying about the incident. When officers said this to Michael Beatty, he became extremely upset, he would shake profusely and while it seemed he would admit to the murder, he would blurt out that he did not do it. As soon as he would blurt this out, he would calm down and be able to resume a normal conversation.

During the interview officers learned that Michael Beatty was supposed to be in District Court in Sanilac County for a hit and run charge on September 15, 1978. A warrant had been issued to the subject for fail to appear and Beatty was notified that they would come down to pick him up. Beatty was advised of this and did not seem upset. He stated at the time of the time of the homicide he was in Diamond City, Arkansas and that several people could verify that he was there. He did procure various people vouching for him being there; however, no one could come up with a specific date as to when he arrived in Diamond City.

Michael Beatty said that approximately a week before John McKinney was murdered McKinney offered him a job. He turned it down because he would have to bath and dress professionally. This being contrary to what he first told Officer Mohr. He said at that time that John McKinney had already hired someone and couldn't hire him.

Office Mohr realized that Beatty had changed his story several times. He changed his story concerning his employment with John McKinney, and also where he was when notified of McKinney's death. And that he was being untruthful on the test questions of the polygraph exam. Apparently Beatty did arrive in Diamond City, Arkansas sometime after the death of John McKinney, but no one could determine definitively when Michael Beatty arrived in Diamond City. The closest it could be pinpointed to when he was there was on September 25, 1977. Officer Mohr concluded that it would have been very easy for Michael Beatty to be involved in the homicide and still be in Diamond City, Arkansas on September 25, 1977.[184]

The investigation concerning the murder of John McKinney was ongoing. On September 7, 1978 Birmingham Police Department received a teletype from Chief Walter Sprenger, of the Holly Police Department, inquiring about the homicide, and whether it had been cleared or not.

Chief Walter Sprenger said he had more information to bring to the table and met with Sergeant Mohr on September 11, 1978 at the Holly Police Department.

Chief Sprenger introduced Sergeant Mohr to a woman named Roberta Laatsch. She stated that when she was a teenager she had lost her parents and was placed in a foster home for a short period of time. The foster home was with Mr and Mrs Milfred Beatty. Mrs Majorie Beatty was the sister of John McKinney, and Michael Beatty was their son. She said she became close to Michael Beatty.

Roberta Laatsch said that it appeared to her that over the past few years Michael Beatty had some sort of mental health issues. She felt he had been regressing mentally to about a ten-year-old. She showed Sergeant Mohr coloring books and other children's articles that Michael Beatty had left at her house. She said that Michael Beatty either spent his time in Michigan, or in Florida, where his parents now lived. He did not have a permanent residence and lived out of the back of his pickup truck.

---

184 Birmingham Police Department, Narrative Report, Follow-up Investigation, Roberta Laatsch Terry Watson and Yvonne McKinney Information, Sergeant Mohr, September 13, 1978.

Roberta Laatsch described Beatty as a grubby and uncleanly person. He would wear the same cloths for three to four weeks, wouldn't bathe and no one really wanted to be around him.

Over the past few years, he had become strongly involved in a Satanic belief. Michael Beatty believed Satan was his guardian angel and that he would scream and yell at her that she was trying to corrupt the world. He also felt that the Indians were going to take over Michigan and go on the war path. She said he was very interested in Indian folk lore and the coloring books and other articles he had were of an Indian historical nature.

Roberta stated that around one month before John McKinney's death, Mr and Mrs Beatty came back to Michigan. They had contacted John McKinney about the possibility of hiring Michael Beatty to work in the gallery. She thought that Michael had an appointment to see John McKinney just prior to McKinney's murder.

Mr and Mrs Beatty were extremely protective of Michael, especially Mrs Beatty. She thought that Mrs Beatty in particular would not give Sergeant Mohr any information regarding Michael.

She said that Michael was a loner and when he traveled to Michigan it was in his pickup truck. She knew that in the past year he had spent approximately one week in Lexington, Michigan and also had spent some time around Gaylord, Michigan, and Port Austin, Michigan. Just recently he was in Saginaw, Michigan. Robert Laatsch stated that the last time she saw Michael was during Labor Day weekend and has not heard from him since. He left several boxes of personal belongings at her home.

The reason she came to investigators was because she believed Michael could have been involved in the homicide of John McKinney, due to his mental health issues. And the fact that he had a job interview right before the murder, and if he was turned down for the job, he might have become extremely upset and possibly violent.

Laatsch said at times Michael Beatty would just and stare into space. And at other times would become very vocal and yell and scream. She had tried to talk to Mrs Beatty about psychiatric care for Michael, but Mrs Beatty didn't feel there was any need because of their Pentecostal beliefs that said the Lord would cure Michael after a period of time.

Roberta Laatsch said that Michael Beatty couldn't hold a job for more than a few days. She thought he might be getting money from his mother, but she couldn't say for sure. Otherwise, she had no idea of where he got his money or how he lived, other than out of the back of his pickup truck. The address that Michael used was on the back of his driver's license, and was that of Mr and Mrs Terry Watson.

Sergeant Mohr contacted Terry Watson on September 12, 1978 and questioned him concerning his relationship with Michael Beatty. Mr Watson stated that Michael had become very strange over the past couple of years. He had grown up with Michael and had known him since kindergarten and that Mr and Mrs Beatty were like second parents to him. But he decided to not let Michael stay at his house because Michael was disrupting the household. And if Michael returned to his house, he was going to tell him he didn't want him there any longer because of this fact.

Terry Watson stated that he felt that Michael Beatty could be capable of harming someone.

Sergeant Mohr contacted Mrs Yvonne McKinney and questioned her about Michael Beatty. She stated that Michael had been to their home several times prior to the homicide, and that Michael Beatty and John McKinney were very close. John did tell her also prior to the homicide that he was thinking about hiring Michael to work at the gallery. Then he decided not to, telling her that it wouldn't be good for business to hire someone like Michael.

Yvonne McKinney also felt that Michael Beatty could be a very violent person. She said she had heard that Michael Beatty went after one of his relatives with a hatchet and attempted to kill the person. She didn't elaborate further on this incident. She also said that approximately six years ago Michael was picked up when he was living in Milford, Michigan with his parents for the rape of a young girl. She was sure it was in Milford.

Sergeant Mohr contacted the Milford Police Department to check on the claim of Mrs McKinney, but they said they didn't have any record of this incident.[185]

Sergeant Mohr and James A'Hearn, special investigator for the Oakland County Prosecutor's office, were assigned to go to Arizona to talk to suspect Douglas Wayne Webster.

The first contact that was made was with a Robert Garelick, owner of an art gallery. Sergeant Mohr had information that at one time Douglass Webster worked for Garelick.

They contacted Garelick at the gallery, and he stated that he had met Webster in the late months of 1976. Webster had gone to Arizona with a letter of recommendation from John McKinney for work. Garelick had known John McKinney for several years when they were both art dealers in Birmingham, Michigan. Mr Webster

---

[185] Detective Malcolm Mohr and Special Investigator for the Oakland Prosecutor's Office James O'Hearn, Narrative Report, Interviews of Douglas Wayne Webster and Lewis Davis, January 13, 1978.

worked for Garelick for approximately three months. He left the employment of Garelick in March of 1977.

Garelick said that Mr Webster was not a good worker and through mutual agreement Webster left the employment of Garelick's gallery. He thought that Douglass Webster had a love relationship going with Reva Yares, of Yares Gallery. However, he had nothing to confirm that.

Investigators questioned Garelick about a subject that was used as an alibi for Douglas Webster named Lewis Davis. Garelick said that Lew Davis was a well-known artist and that most of the dealings of Davis were through Yares Gallery.

Garelick stated that a couple of years ago he was having an Indian show at John McKinney's Birmingham Gallery and it appeared strange to him that at closing times men would come to visit McKinney. At around closing time McKinney would escort the men upstairs and this would be about the time that Garelick would leave the gallery.

Investigators said that Doug Webster had told investigators that Garelick could verify where Webster was on the weekend of the homicide. Garelick said this wasn't true, and he couldn't figure out why Webster would use him as an alibi, because he hadn't seen Webster for approximately five months prior to the homicide.

Garelick was shown a composite of the unknown female that was supposed to have had lunch with John McKinney the day of the homicide, but he was unable to identify this person.

On Saturday, January 14, 1978, investigators drove to Pinnacle Peak. After checking around, investigators located Lewis Davis who lived on the side of the mountain. Davis was very cooperative with investigators. He said he had met Douglas Webster through

Reva Yares. He was questioned as to possible connections between Douglas Webster and Reva Yares and he was emphatic that there was not a romantic relationship between the two. And in fact, Reva Yares was his lover.

    Lewis Davis also stated that he could verify Webster's alibi as to being in Scottsdale, Arizona at the time of the homicide.

Investigators contacted Douglas Webster's attorney. His attorney was reluctant to have Webster take the polygraph exam. She said she had been advised that there were no reliable polygraph operators in the state of Arizona. Investigators assured the attorney that there were competent polygraph operators in Phoenix, Arizona that worked for the Department of Public Safety and were well known throughout Arizona.[186]

On September 19, 1977 Sergeant Mohr and Detective Marble went to talk to Martin Hoogasian, who was an artist and had several pieces of his work exhibited at McKinney's Birmingham Gallery. He said he was aware of Linda Webster and also the relationship with Shirley Essex Phillips.

    He stated McKinney was into a type of magical practice that he termed "Don Juan." He also said that there were secret letters and writings from Doug Webster to John McKinney.

    He knew that John McKinney was bisexual and stated that John admitted he had a relationship with a man named Mike Miller who was a teacher at Groves High School.[187]

---

[186] Sergeant Mohr and Detective Winkelman, Narrative Report, Interview of Martin Hoogasian, September 19, 1977.
[187] Detectives Marble and Winkelman, Narrative Report, Information from Douglas Courtmer, September 23, 1977.

On September 23, 1977, Detectives Marble and Winkelman started to check on Bowen Brock's and Shirley Essex Phillip's stories regarding their amorous liason at the Somerset Inn. They checked with Douglas Courtmer, the assistant manager of Somerset Inn, in regards to a room being rented by Bowen Brock. Room 229 was allegedly rented between 11:30 am and 12:00 pm under the names of Brock and Greenwald. Mr Courtmer could not find the receipts for this transaction and said his bookkeeper was away on holiday. He explained that they had a very large backlog of receipts.[188]

John McKinney's son, John Mark McKinney, went to investigators to talk about possible drug activity on the part of his deceased father. John suspected his father was involved in some type of drug activity because of a couple of large bank deposits that were made and these deposits were made around last Christmas. He then said he had a conversation about narcotics with his father which strengthened his suspicion. John said he had once asked to borrow $40 from his father and his father had replied, "What are you going to do? Buy a hit of mescaline?" This information concerning his suspected narcotics activity was also relayed to Mr McKinney's CPA. John said at one time he found his father and Doug Webster at the gallery and they were both very high. He had no concrete proof though, if he was involved in hard narcotics.

  Detectives asked him who he thought killed his father. He then mumbled something like, "You don't kill people unless you

---

[188] Detectives Solomon and Marble, Narrative Report, Interview of John Mark McKinney, September 27, 1977.

have insurance or if you have some information that people want or don't want you to talk about."[189]

Sergeant Mohr interviewed a gallery employee who stated that being a bookkeeper in his business he was aware of the fact that John McKinney was very lax in his book work. This is in contrast to what Yvonne McKinney had said regarding her husband's bookkeeping. She said he was very meticulous in his book work.[190]

Officer Fraser had observed the body of John McKinney and took copious notes. He described the victim, John McKinney, as lying on his back with an arm underneath him, while his legs were straight out with one leg crossed over the other. There was a large amount of blood underneath the subject's head, also on the wall just right of the body. McKinney was dressed in blue jeans, a blue jean jacket and brown suede shoes. The jacket appeared to have been soaked in blood. Lying just to the right of the victim was a key ring with two keys on it. Fire Chief Nunnelley advised Officer Fraser that the victim may have been injured upstairs as there was a large amount of blood on the upstairs second floor area of the building. They both walked up the stairs observing the blood on the carpet and the stairway. There was also blood at the top of the stairway. Officer Fraser then went to McKinney's office on the northwest side of the building. There was blood on the wall near a window. And a pair of brown plastic frame glasses on the floor on the south side of the room. Near the desk at the north end of the room there was a lens on the floor, which appeared to have come from the

---

189 Sergeant Mohr, Narrative Report, September 27, 1977.
190 Birmingham Police Department, Narrative Report, Detective Fraser, Crime Scene Homicide Investigation of John McKinney, September 20, 1977.

brown frame glasses, as there was a lens missing. On a bookcase on the south side of the room there were two glasses filled with a purple-colored liquid.[191]

The forensic lab determined that John McKinney was shot by a .22 caliber, Remington-Peters brand revolver with gold tone bullets. The rifling specifications, although somewhat distorted, appear to be 8 lands and 8 grooves with a right-hand twist. The specifications were consistent with many foreign manufactured revolvers (example, German Valor) however, no suspected firearm should be overlooked, according to Michael Arrowood, laboratory specialist.[192]

On September 29, 1977 Investigator A'Hearn had a long conversation with an individual concerning victim John McKinney. This person knew that John McKinney was dating someone's wife and that they had taken a trip to Lake Erie together.

The interviewee asked Investigator A'Hearn if he knew that the moon was red on Monday night.

"You probably don't but on the way down to Toledo I was looking at the moon and it was red."

"Does that mean something to you?"

"Of course."

"What does it mean to you?"

"Well, I just look at the moon and I say I see it is red, actually I don't know what it meant. But looked at the moon and said gee it is red; it's a usual thing when it is red and round or full

---

[191] State of Michigan, Regional Crime Detection Laboratory, Laboratory Report, Homicide, John McKinney, Firearms, October 5, 1977.
[192] State of Michigan, Regional Crime Detection Laboratory.

or whatever a half moon and I wondered what does it mean to me, I don't know, so now that John's dead I suppose that it had some kind of relationship like that. Last night it was red too," he laughed, "As a matter of fact on the way back I saw two over turned trucks which is unusual in the summertime. That was probably a weird time, I say that because John was writing a lot about energy. I don't have the faintest idea about what that means. I know that about like a year or two ago he spent some time on an island off of the Georgia, North Carolina or South Carolina coast. It is a funded thing where somebody suggests you to these people and they say we are gonna give you some money and two-or-three weeks' time to come down here to do whatever it is you wanted to do with your time, and he was writing on energy."

He then brought up a person who had traveled with John McKinney the previous year, and that he should talk to this person about what type of energy McKinney was interested in.

Investigator A'Hearn asked this person about a particular piece of art. This art piece was signed Cigler 77 with a slash through it. The interviewee did not have the faintest idea who the artist was. A'Hearn said they couldn't find the artist of this piece anywhere. The art was identified as a batik.

"As far as leads go, have you got any?" asked the interviewee.

"Well, that's not the way we investigate things, we keep the secrets and we ask you the questions." said A'Hearn.[193]

---

[193] Birmingham Police Department, Narrative Report, Detective Solomon, Re-Construction of Crime Scene, September 21, 1977.

After the MSP had finished processing the crime scene, Sergeant Mohr and Detective Solomon went upstairs to reconstruct the crime scene. They attempted to trace the pattern of a bullet, and found several suspected holes on the far wall; however, none of them matched up.

Detectives felt that if the bullet ricocheted off the wall it might have landed some place on the floor. They found the slug on the fourth step from the bottom. The forensic team photographed the evidence. It appeared to be a .22 or .25 caliber lead cartridge that was was completely mangled and twisted as if it had hit a blunt object. They went back to the second floor and tried to determine the trajectory of the slug and where it may have hit the wall causing it to fall on the stairway below. They thought that this particular shot was fired from outside of the office in the lobby area.[194]

On September 26, 1977 Shirley Essex Phillips took a polygraph at the Northville, MSP crime lab. She was presented with several baseline questions before the test was administered.

"Who do you admire the most?"

"My husband." she said.

"Who do you admire the least, or disrespect?"

"Richard Nixon." she replied.

"What was the worst hurt feeling you've ever experienced?"

"John McKinney's death."

"What brings up your most positive or best feelings?"

"Many things."

---

[194] Birmingham Police Department, Narrative Report, Detective Solomon, Polygraph of Shirley Essex Phillips, September 26, 1977.

The polygrapher then began asking questions pertaining to the homicide. She denied having any knowledge of as to who planned the murder. She was asked if she was in love with John McKinney and she said yes. But added it was an emotional type of love and not physical. She was then asked if they had made love and she said no. However, they had hugged and kissed at one time, which she said was a common greeting among close friends.

She said she did spend the afternoon at the Somerset Inn with Mr Bowen Brock and she was in the area of Bonwit-Tellers at the Somerset Mall at approximately 2:40 pm. Then directly after going to the mall she went to meet Mr Brock in room 229. She said it was before 3:00 pm and she had spent some time in the lobby waiting for him. They were in the hotel from 3:00 pm to 7:00 pm.

Detectives then confronted her with the fact that they had checked at the motel to verify her claims previously and found out from the maid service that that particular room was clean and vacant. She denied that claim and said that wasn't the case. At one point in time a maid had knocked on the door, but they didn't let the maid in. She couldn't remember the exact time though.

Shirley Essex Phillips told detectives that John McKinney had said to her during a phone conversation that, "When you get divorced, everybody is going to be surprised when we get married and stay close." That was the last conversation she had with John McKinney.

Shirley Essex Phillips said that John McKinney had come to her house quite often for dinner and on several occasions had told her that he was in love with her. These dinners at the house included Shirley, her husband, and John McKinney. On many occasions her husband, Mr Phillips, would have to leave after dinner and John McKinney would stay at the house. She believed that John was wrestling in his mind with his feelings for Linda Webster. She was asked if she thought Linda was capable of killing John and she said she didn't know.[195]

Detective Solomon went to speak to a friend of John McKinney named Dr Herman Schornstein, a psychiatrist. Dr Schornstein stated that he had known John since 1960; however, the relationship with him in the last seventeen years has been strictly on the business level. He didn't know anything about his personal life. Dr Schornstein was connected with the Little Gallery run by Peggy DeSalle and he knew John through this gallery.

The doctor's alibi the day of John McKinney's homicide was that Tuesday he was working at the Oakland County Child Consulting Center in Pontiac from 9:00 am until 5:00 pm and he went straight home after that. He had been watching the 6 o'clock news when he heard the news report. On that particular Tuesday night at 7:00 pm a meeting was scheduled in Birmingham at the Personal and Family Adjustment Center. Dr Shornstein was medical director at this clinic. This 7:00 pm staff meeting on Tuesday night was for the purpose of installing John McKinney on the Board of Directors.

The doctor was asked when he last saw or spoke to John McKinney and he replied that last fall he saw him at an art gallery opening at Cranbrook and hadn't seen him since. However, in September of 1976 Dr Schornstein saw John McKinney in London where they both happened to be on vacation. As the doctor was crossing a street in downtown London he saw John McKinney on

---

[195] Birmingham Police Department, Narrative Report, Detective Solomon, Interview of Dr Herman Schornstein, September 27, 1977.

the other side of the street and briefly spoke with him. He didn't know who McKinney was with in London at that time since they were both en route to engagements and only spoke momentarily.

Dr Schornstein suggested that detectives check with Peggy DeSalle at the Little Gallery as she supposedly knew John very well. The doctor said he recently learned that Peggy DeSalle had helped McKinney finance his home in Troy, Michigan.

Dr Schornstein also told detectives that John McKinney used to pick up Peggy DeSalle and the two of them would go together to the Detroit Art Dealers Association meetings. Peggy DeSalle told the doctor she enjoyed going to these meetings with John McKinney because she would always sit in the front passenger side on top of John's Bible. Apparently she got a kick out of this, stating that John never went anywhere without his Bible.[196]

On September 21, 1977, Joel Smith, reporter for *The Detroit News*, stated he had heard rumors that John McKinney had contacts with the underworld. He said John McKinney had spent Sundays at the Bloomfield Hills Nursing Home at Square Lake and Woodward Avenue. Smith said the nursing home, according to his sources, was operated by Lenny Schultz, who was a noted underworld person. Smith also mentioned that McKinney had contacts with Garelick Studio.

On September 23, 1977, Mr Bryan Knez, an attorney, wanted to come in and discuss Linda Webster with detectives. He felt he had information that might be pertinent to the investigation.

---

[196] Birmingham Police Department, Narrative Report, Sergeant Mohr, September 27, 1977.

He said Linda Webster worked for him for approximately four months, starting in September 10, 1976, and left his employment on February of 1977. During this time he had learned of Linda's association with John McKinney and it appeared that Linda Webster was very much in love with him. He stated that several times John McKinney would call Linda Webster at the office and break dates with her and then she would be depressed the rest of the day. He said that it wasn't uncommon for this scenario to happen at least two times per week.

According to Mr Knez, that even though Linda Webster was allegedly very much in love with John McKinney, she was also going out with other men while she was dating McKinney. He said that he didn't believe Linda Webster had a drinking problem; however, she was drinking all the time, but in his opinion she was not considered an alcoholic.

Mr Knez felt she was desperate for male companionship. And that the relationship with John McKinney was what broke up the marriage between her and her now ex-husband, Doug Webster.

Linda Webster had a close associate who worked directly across the hall from Knez's law office. This person was Shirley Yater, who worked at Data Products. Mr Knez said that several times after John would break a date with Linda, she would contact Shirley Yater and they would go out for the evening. He also said that Linda was borrowing money from Shirley Yater.

Detectives decided to go speak to Shirley Yater across the hall at Data Products. Shirley explained that she and Linda became close friends when worked across the hall; however, she hadn't seen Linda in about five months. She stated she was aware of the fact that Linda Webster was going out with John McKinney and thought she was very much in love with him, and John did break dates with her several times. But, she added, Linda was not going out with other men while she was dating John.

It appeared to Sergeant Mohr that after the homicide of John McKinney, Linda Webster, Cary Wilkie and another [redacted] individual had been together a few times to discuss the situation. It was discovered that the [redacted] individual had called Yvonne McKinney, and Linda and Douglas Webster, after the murder to find out what was going to happen to the art gallery.

Linda Webster had mentioned to detectives that she was extremely upset due to the fact the car keys of John McKinney were missing. She said that she was upset because along with the car keys on the same ring was a key to her apartment. When she was questioned as to how she knew the car keys were missing, she said that a [redacted] individual had told her. When questioned on how this [redacted] individual knew this, she said that Yvonne McKinney had told him about the missing car keys.[197]

On the afternoon of September 27, 1977, Detectives Chambers and Solomon interviewed a Mrs Freda Riccardo. Freda knew John McKinney because she was a part-time employee at the gallery and did secretarial work. She said she knew John for approximately three years. The last time she saw John was the weekend of September 2, 1977, just before he went on a trip to New York. She said she ran the gallery while John was in New York.

---

197 Birmingham Police Department, Narrative Report, Interview of Freda Riccardo, Detective Solomon, 3:45 pm, September 27, 1997.

When asked about the wine in the gallery, she said it was common for artists while they were in the gallery to go upstairs and have a glass of wine and browse through a book in the lobby area. However, this was never done in his office on the second floor. She also said John McKinney told her that he wouldn't allow any marijuana smoking in the gallery.

Detectives asked her if she knew Shirley Essex Phillips, and she stated that she had met her twice and saw her again at the funeral. Freda thought it was strange that after the funeral on Saturday Shirley called Freda at home. Shirley wondered about Freda's involvement in the case and asked if she had been questioned by detectives yet. Shirley Essex Phillips told Freda that the two of them should get together for lunch soon and wanted to call her in the evening after she was questioned by detectives. Freda couldn't understand Shirley's interest in her all of a sudden and Shirley's interest in the detectives questioning her about the homicide.

Freda was told on one occasion never to tell Linda anything that went on between John McKinney and Shirley Essex Phillips.

It became evident that Freda was aware of the love triangle and all the people involved, such as Bowen Brock, Shirley Essex Phillips and Linda Webster. She said she figured this out by over hearing conversations in the gallery.

Freda felt that John McKinney was hiding something in the gallery. Her reasoning for this was that all of the part-time people who worked for him only worked a few days per week; however, the work load in the gallery appeared to be enough for a full time employee. She thought there was something in the gallery that John McKinney was hiding and didn't want an employee to become too familiar with. She was questioned as to whether or not she had any knowledge of a safe on the premises and she stated she did not.

Freda told detectives she reads tea leaves as a hobby and John McKinney was becoming very interested in her reading these tea leaves. She said that John believed in extrasensory perception (ESP) and telepathic powers. She said John McKinney had strong feelings regarding the occult and he insisted that John Blanchard have his tea leaves read by Freda.

Freda said they had an art show at the gallery that year and the art show was called the "Boyd Warner American Indian Show," and John McKinney was not at this show because he was attending his aunt's funeral. However, Ronald Frey and another individual were in the gallery. Freda stated that she was a little upset that day over something that had to do with her wages and had gone upstairs to sit down in the lobby to relax. Ronald Frey approached her and told her to have a glass of wine, which she refused. She said then Frey sat on the floor in front of her, in front of the chair that she was sitting in, and he put his hands on her waist and said to her, "You turn me on." She became very upset over this and told him to leave and that she was old enough to be his mother. She got up and walked away and there were no more advances made to her by Ronald Frey. She said at that time Frey was drinking white wine.

On one occasion while Freda was reading tea leaves she said to John McKinney that he would be looking for an apartment soon and that he and an associate looked at each other in a very strange way.

She kept emphasizing to the investigators that there was such a degree of trust between John McKinney and this associate like she has never seen before.

Freda was asked if she could identify a photograph of a piece of tapestry that was missing from the gallery. She looked at this photograph and identified the missing property as a wrapping. She said this was hanging on a wall in the gallery and that it was worth approximately $900.00.[198]

On September 26, 1977 Detectives Mohr and Solomon were attempting to locate the source of two pieces of cloth art work that were found in the center of John McKinney's desk the morning the body was found. No one at the gallery or associated with the gallery could advise where the art work was from. The investigators contacted a person knowledgeable about various genres of artistic style who stated the art work was called batik. The person did not recognize the art work and did not recognize the signature, Cigler, on the bottom of the art work. She showed the artwork to various other people who might recognize the artist or the art work, but no one recognized it.

The detectives then proceeded to visit the Birmingham/Bloomfield Art Association and talked to several people in the office area who were familiar with batik. However, no one recognized the name Cigler.

Sergeant Mohr contacted the MSP in regards to Ronald Frey. This person had been mentioned several times as a possible suspect. The only information Mohr had on Ronald Frey was that he had a studio named Schoolhaus Studio in Kalkaska, Michigan. Sergeant Harger from the MSP called Mohr back and said he had talked to neighbors

---

[198] Birmingham Police Department, Narrative Report, Sergeant Mohr, September 27, 1977.

in the area and they said they had not seen Ron Frey the weekend of the 24th of September, and they did not recall if he was in the area the weekend of the homicide. However, they said that he did drive a green American Motors car.

Sergeant Mohr and Lieutenant Kalbfleisch interviewed Dr Henry Phillips, the husband of Shirley Essex Phillips. He said he had known John McKinney for nineteen years. But he had only known him personally for two years. He gave an alibi for the date of the homicide detailing his time from 8:15 am to up until midnight. Dr Phillips said that as far as he knew, John McKinney only drank white wine, and only drank red when white was not available. White wine was available in the refrigerator next to the bottle of red wine. Officer Mohr noted that the two glasses found in the gallery office during the investigation of the physical evidence contained red wine.

Dr Phillips stated that John McKinney was the one who talked him into going up north where he found his wife with Bowen Brock. John had advised him that he was working too hard and that he should just let things go for a while and go up north to their cottage and be with his wife. So he took his advice and went to the cottage only to find his wife cheating on him.

Detectives found out that Dr Phillips was in the Air Force Rangers and they had taught him how to kill. He said he had punched Brock once and when Brock got up it was Dr Phillips intention to use the heel of his hand to break Brock's nose. He said he was taught this in his military training. He knocked Brock down a second time and was going to kick him when Shirley started screaming.

Brock Bowen did sustain a broken nose and it appeared as if he had been kicked severely.

Dr Phillips stated that he had a feeling that John McKinney was having an affair with his wife, but he had nothing to substantiate this. However, he did tell John McKinney that he would rather have him having an affair with his wife than Bowen Brock.

On September 25, 1977 Sergeant Mohr talked to an auxiliary police officer from the Birmingham Police Department, Ken Staples and his wife Elizabeth. They said they had known John and Yvonne McKinney personally. They also knew Linda Webster. It appeared to them that John McKinney and Linda Webster were very much in love and that John had talked several times about getting a divorce.

Mr and Mrs Staples felt that John McKinney and Doug Webster were bisexual and that possibly the triangle between John, Doug, and Linda was a sexual thing. They also stated that John was getting into religion so strongly that it was almost becoming and occult type of thing.[199]

Investigators interviewed Martin Hoogasian who had known John McKinney for approximately seven years. He was questioned for his general knowledge of John McKinney and his character. He thought that McKinney had sexual relations with Shirley Essex Phillips. He said that McKinney went to New York about two weeks ago and he had told him that he was going with Shirley Essex Phillips and Dr Phillips was paying for the trip.

---

199 Birmingham Police Department, Narrative Report, Interview of Martin Hoogasian, Sergeant Mohr, September 27, 1977.

John McKinney told Martin Hoogasian that he was having problems between Shirley and Linda. He also stated that Linda could not understand the relationship with Shirley Essex Phillips. McKinney told Hoogasian that he could not go to New York with Shirley Essex Phillips because they would wind up in bed together.

Hoogasian said that he was positive that John was bisexual. And that McKinney admitted to him that he was having an affair with a man by the name of Mike Miller. He also believed that he was having homosexual relations with Doug Webster. Another possible homosexual involvement was with a Cranbrook Institute employee by the name of Gary Knodel. Hoogasian also thought that McKinney might be involved with the Director of the Birmingham/Bloomfield Art Association. And there was another individual named Bob Kidd that McKinney was sexually involved with. Bob Kidd had a boyfriend named Ray Fleming.

Hoogasian said that just two weeks ago John McKinney was talking about getting married to Linda Webster.

Martin Hoogasian also said that John McKinney was involved in "Don Juan" magic, and Doug Webster was also involved in this occult activity. Apparently this is a kind of magic with the mind and McKinney had talked to him about this. McKinney told him that he and Doug Webster were "simulated" by crows. In other words, they could change, or shape shift into this type of bird.[200]

On September 28, 1977, Detectives met with Joy Colby, a *Detroit News* freelance writer. Her specialty for the newspaper was art. Joy

---

200 Birmingham Detective Bureau, Detectives Chambers and Solomon, Interview of Joy Colby, 4:10 pm, September 28, 1977.

Colby had known John McKinney for at least twenty-five years. She had met him through Peggy DeSalle of the Little Gallery when he was a framer. Joy Colby didn't know anything about John McKinney's professional education just that when she met him he was a framer and she felt he didn't have a great eye for art. She said most of his shows weren't first rate. It was her understanding that when Sally Saunders and John McKinney left the Little Gallery, John concentrated on the framing and Sally on the exhibitions. Then the exhibitions went down in quality after Sally left. Joy Colby felt he had an informal knowledge of art that he had picked up here and there.

"But there is such a thing as an eye too, and I can't say that he had a great eye." said Colby.

"I understand it perfectly." said Detective Chambers.

He seemed very gentle and kind, but, said Joy Colby, John impressed her as a very strange man.

She was quite mystified at the idea of letting Bob Garelick use the gallery to give exhibitions. Bob Garelick had had a gallery in Birmingham and went out to Scottsdale, Arizona. John McKinney let Bob Garelick use the gallery as a kind of shop, bringing work in to sell. Joy Colby didn't know what kind of arrangement they had but she said good galleries just didn't do that type of thing. Galleries have their own point of view, she explained, and they don't invite someone in to show their work in that fashion.

She said that McKinney later brought an exhibition of Indian work that Bob Garelick had sent from Scottsdale, which seemed very peculiar. They then began hearing rumors in the art community that Garelick was going to move back to Detroit.

"Was that Indian work recent?" said Detective Chambers.

"It was last spring sometime." she replied.

"Was that the Boyd Warner Indian Show?"

"Exactly, yes. It was the kind of stuff that was very touristy. Stuff that you can get out in Arizona by the car load and there really didn't seem to be any reason for having that there. It was a very strange operation and I must say I did wonder at the time whether John was in some sort of financial need."

Detective Chambers asked Joy Colby if she had any knowledge of John's interest in Egyptian history. She said no, but there was an artist named Robert Nipshod who had a show in McKinney's gallery that was a specialist in Egypt. Colby said he was a very, very good painter. And he had a one-man show. This was about two years ago.

Joy Colby stated that there was a religious service given by Reverend Richard Myers that was very upsetting. She said the reverend said that John had joined the church either a month or week ago, something within that short time span, and *he had put him aside*. It was a very cryptic remark. He had said this apparently not knowing what would happen to him, and a day later he was dead.

She further elaborated that the reverend had kept making references to John McKinney being neither in heaven or in hell, as if there was some kind of dark, strange and forbidding thing going on.[201]

On September 27, 1977, Detectives Chambers and Solomon interviewed Marie Meredith, who worked at the Little Gallery in Birmingham, Michigan. She had known John McKinney for about

---

[201] Birmingham Detective Bureau, Detectives Chambers and Solomon, Interview of Marie Meredith, 1:30 pm, September 27, 1977.

seventeen years. She described herself as a painter and a draftsman. Marie Meredith said that John McKinney kept encouraging her in her art and he was one of the people that got one of her drawings into the Detroit Institute of Art drawing shows. It was one of their very first drawing shows, she said.

    Detectives asked Marie Meredith when was the last time she had stopped by John McKinney's Birmingham Gallery. She said that it was after her vacation; she came back to work and ran by the gallery just to see what was on the walls and to ask him how business was. He was in very good spirits and said business was very good through the summer. He told her that he had spent a week in Georgia again. There is a sea island off of the coast of Georgia which is owned by Mrs Clifford West — Sandy West. He said he had gone down there for a week during the summer. And the year before or two years before he had spent two weeks down there on the island. He said he had down a lot of riding. Apparently you have your own room or cabin or whatever type of secluded arrangement that was provided where you are away from everyone and you only get together in the evenings or something like that. She said he had gone down there to meditate. Marie Meredith said he had spoken of that time in a strange kind of way, as if he had been in touch with a cosmic something or other. She never understood that part of the story.[202]

On September 30, 1977, Detectives Marble and Solomon went to the Little Gallery to speak with Peggy DeSalle. She had known John McKinney since 1953 when he started at the gallery as a

---

[202] Birmingham Police Department, Narrative Report, Interview of Peggy DeSalle, Detectives Marble and Solomon, October 11, 1977.

framer. He had come up to Michigan from Little Rock, Arkansas. She said McKinney had worked for her until 1968 when he and Sally Saunders left the Little Gallery and opened up the Birmingham Gallery on Haynes Street.

Detectives asked Mrs DeSalle if she helped finance McKinney's new gallery. She said no but she thought that John's brother may have helped with the financing. She also thought the Saunders' helped with the financing.

Peggy DeSalle stated that her deceased husband was very fond of John McKinney and was instrumental in teaching McKinney what he knew of the art field. According to Mrs DeSalle her husband was a very intelligent man and quite polished in the arts. She described John McKinney as being very naive, not knowing anything about art work, and he spoke with a southern accent. She said he had no formal education and anything that he learned about proper speech and etiquette and the art field was taught to him by the DeSalles. Peggy DeSalle stated that her husband in fact treated John as if he were a son.[203]

On October 27, 1977 Detectives Mohr and Studt took Yvonne McKinney to the Northville State Police post for a polygraph test. The polygraph examiner advised Sergeant Mohr that Yvonne McKinnney knew nothing of the homicide.

She did mention to Detective Mohr that she had been to a psychic in regards to the homicide a few days ago. The psychic advised her of several things about the homicide she was unaware

---

[203] Birmingham Police Department, Narrative Report, Sergeant Mohr, October 28, 1977.

of. Detective Mohr obtained information about the psychic, Mrs Helen Edwards, and made an appointment to speak with her.

Mrs Edwards did not follow a logical sequential sequence of events, but spoke to Sergeant Mohr of how the information presented itself to her. She said the subject they were looking for is someone they least expect to have committed the crime; however, they were checking into him at the present time. She said John McKinney was homosexual and there was marijuana somehow involved in the killing.

Mrs Edwards said John McKinney owed someone a lot of money and the incident happened on Monday night. She said that they were checking on a man at the present time and it is the right man. The subject they were looking for is a very prominent man and well liked.

Helen Edwards also stated that they had not even begun to touch the surface of John McKinney, indicating that all the facts they had on McKinney was just the start. She said his activities were not on the up and up, and that John McKinney *was very much like the child killer*, in reference to the OCCK case.

Mrs Edwards said John McKinney was in New York and possibly the subject they were looking for might have something to do with the East Coast. He knew the man who he lead into the building and that they were going to tie his hands but they did not have a chance. McKinney's girlfriend was not involved in the murder but there was another woman involved.

She said he had promised someone something and that he did not fulfill his obligation. He was friends with many police officers, but there was an ulterior motive to this, possibly to get information for some other purpose.[204]

Sergeant Mohr contacted Robert Garelick in Scottsdale, Arizona and asked if could provide an alibi for Douglas Webster. A report issued by Arizona Intelligence stated that Douglas Webster used Robert Garelick as an alibi for the weekend the homicide took place. Mr Garelick stated he could not provide an alibi for Douglas Webster and this was untrue.

Sergeant Mohr then contacted Arizona Intelligence and talked to Sergeant Bullard and discussed the situation with him. Mohr said that Douglas Webster and the owner of Yares Gallery, Reva Yares, might be boyfriend and girlfriend. Sergeant Bullard stated that on the initial background check of Doug Webster he felt that this was a strong possibility. Sergeant Mohr thought that it would be likely then that Reva Yares might fabricate a story stating that Doug Webster was in Arizona at the time of the homicide. Taking into consideration the fact that Garelick stated he had no knowledge of Webster being in Arizona at the time of the homicide.

Linda Webster told Sergeant Mohr that Doug Webster had a valuable scroll and that it was from the Peterson family. The scroll belonged to John McKinney and it was priceless. John McKinney had loaned it to Douglas Webster.

Sergeant Mohr followed up on this information and found that the scroll came from a Thomas Peterson whom he then contacted. Thomas Peterson stated that yes, there was a Coptic

---

204 Birmingham Police Department, Narrative Report, Follow-up Investigation, Sergeant Mohr, October 26, 1977.

scroll that Peterson had purchased in Ethiopia, approximately a year ago. He had purchased it in a rural area from a native of Ethiopia for only $5.00. This scroll was given to John McKinney as a gift and it was written in a language that they were unable to as of yet to translate. The scroll was approximately 4 inches wide by 7 feet long and made of parchment. Mr Peterson stated he had no knowledge as to the actual value of the scroll.[205]

Sergeant Mohr continued with the further investigation of suspect Douglas Webster. General conclusions could be drawn concerning the suspect. Approximately one and a half years ago Webster was a business partner with John McKinney. At some point in time during the partnership there was a romance between McKinney and Douglas Webster's wife, Linda Webster. Shortly after that the suspect and his wife broke up and Douglas Webster moved out of the Birmingham Gallery. Douglas Webster then left the state and was paid for his portion of shares in the gallery by McKinney. Birmingham Police Department was in possession of letters confirming that the business ties were severed and completely paid off by the victim.

    The alibis of Douglas Webster regarding the homicide of John McKinney were also suspect. It was thought that Reva Yares, of Yares Gallery was possibly involved with the suspect and therefore might possibly cover for Webster being in Scottsdale, Arizona during the time of the homicide of John McKinney. Also there was the fact that Robert Garelick, of Garelick's Gallery, could not verify Douglas Webster's presence in Scottsdale and hadn't

---

[205] Birmingham Police Department, Narrative Report, To Department of Public Safety Intelligence Division, Phoenix, Arizona, Sergeant Malcolm Mohr, November 4, 1977.

seen him for approximately five months prior to the homicide. Although Garelick stated that he did run into Douglas Webster in the post office approximately one week after the homicide.

The outward appearance portrayed by Douglas Webster of the cordial severing of his business relationship with John McKinney proved to be a fallacious. After interviewing several people it was felt there were hard feelings between Webster and McKinney, and Sergeant Mohr felt there was sufficient motive for Douglas Webster to commit the murder.

There was also the intriguing enigma of John McKinney and Douglas Webster being involved in a possible magic cult or something of that nature that people termed "Don Juan." It was known that both subjects were strongly involved in the cult.[206]

On October 31, 1977 Detectives Marble and Winkelmann met with the psychic, Mrs Helen Edwards, to walk through Birmingham Gallery and obtain information in regards to the homicide of John McKinney. This was a continuation of a meeting that had involved Mrs Edwards and the detectives to gain further insight and impressions of the murder.

Her first impression upon entering the gallery was that John McKinney was backed into a corner. She felt there was money or something removed. And there were two wallets, one wallet contained little money and another wallet contained a lot of money and there was money taken.

She then asked the detectives if they had found drugs. They answered no, just marijuana.

---

[206] Birmingham Police Department, Narrative Report, Detectives Winkelmann and Marble, Psychic Helen Edwards, October 31, 1977.

She said that John was in big trouble. That somebody with an "A" like Adam in his name was involved in the actual murder...deeper into something evil.

She said there was another lady. They were paying or talking about drugs. There was an argument in the upstairs office. At this time the detectives and Helen Edwards entered the office and she stated that things had been changed in the room. Which was correct. The table that was against the east wall had been moved to the center of the room. And the other table that was being used as a desk that had been placed along the west wall at the north end of the room had been moved the opposite way. She said she could see an argument in the office and there was a connection with Ohio and Georgia.

Helen Edwards asked Mrs McKinney if her husband was a gambler or a go-between for some type of transaction. Mrs McKinney said no. Mrs Edwards said that the business was a front for something else. And that John was a homosexual. That he owed money, had a lot of money and that money was taken. That the subject involved had long hair and had come for money.

Then Helen Edwards asked who was Marge. Mrs McKinney replied that was John's sister. Mrs Edwards stated that Marge thought that John could do no wrong.

She told detectives to check the files of people that they knew of and of also relating to Mrs McKinney. She said there is a file of people you least expect.

Mrs Edwards asked Mrs McKinney if she was receiving any funny phone calls where a subject would not speak or that there would be a very short conversation and then they would hang up. Mrs McKinney said yes, she had received some strange phone calls where nobody would talk and the line would be be open, or someone would question her and it would be a very short conversation, such as wrong number, etc.

She then asked Mrs McKinney if she looked in the floor safe. Mrs McKinney said she did not know where it was. Helen Edwards said she could see a carpet or something over the safe.

She said the murder had something to do with a 6, but she could not determine if it was a date or something else regarding a 6. But she said that in her mind a 6 meant something incomplete or unfinished. Helen Edwards said there was something that was hidden.

Mrs Edwards then asked if John was more of an artist or a devil. Mrs McKinney said a little bit of both. Helen Edwards said she could see someone twisting John's arm in the work room on the second level where the framing was actually done. She said I see a partner, Douglas Webster; talk to him, she said to detectives, answers are still to be given by him. She then stated I feel heavy like I am going to be sick and she wanted to get out of the room.

They then went downstairs. Mrs Edwards went to a desk in the rear room and sat down. While sitting there she said she saw a man come to the door. John McKinney knew the man and opened this door. The man then struck him possibly with an object and drove him half way into the other room.

She then walked back into the gallery and asked if John was sadistic. Yvonne McKinney said she thought possibly somewhat. Helen Edwards said she could see him and that he like to see people suffer.

She then went to the downstairs office again and standing where John McKinney was found asked if this was where the body was discovered. The answer was in the affirmative. She then described how the body was lying on the floor.

John McKinney had other things to do, said Helen Edwards, but he knew that man that was at the door so he opened it. McKinney had wanted to change his clothes and get to a meeting. He was also going to see someone after this meeting and wouldn't be home until one or two o'clock in the morning, is what he had in mind.

The man at the door had light hair that was long. And the woman he was with had natural hair that was dark but was dyed or bleached. The woman was not the murderer, but was at the scene.[207]

On November 23, 1977, Sergeant Mohr contacted Mr Bill Rosso, building owner of the Birmingham gallery. He contacted him for the purpose of attempting to locate a floor safe that was mentioned by the psychic, Helen Edwards. Mr Rosso showed Sergeant Mohr a floor safe underneath the carpeting. It was noted at this time that the major portion of the floor safe was covered by a petition in the wall that Mrs McKinney stated was constructed when they were moving into the building. Sergeant Mohr thought that due to the carpeting not being pulled away and the petition being installed over the floor safe, that the floor safe had not been used since the Birmingham gallery had been established in the building.[208]

Psychiatrist Bruce Danto received a phone call from an individual who used to work for John McKinney in his art studio and shop in Birmingham. He said he had taped an interview for the Birminham Police Department, but had not discussed suspicions with the police about a possible connection to the OCCK. Since he

---

207 Birmingham Police Department, Narrative Report, Sergeant Malcolm Mohr, December 2, 1977.
208 Bruce L. Danto M.D., Letter to Birmingham Police Department, September 22, 1977.

had seen Dr Danto on TV and had heard him on the radio he felt it would be easier to talk to him rather than the police. He told Danto that he did not recall any child pornography in the gallery but McKinney did keep a private file and had a safe or vault near his desk.[209]

On December 12, 1997 Sergeant Mohr was contacted by phone by Yvonne McKinney who wanted to confer with him about an important matter. He went to Birmingham Gallery to meet with her and she said that in going through the belongings and inventory records, etc., that she found that there was something of value missing. She said the item that was missing was a Guttenberg Bible. She stated that this Bible, according to the people she spoke with, was worth $ 2,000,000.00 and that at one time it was in the possession of John McKinney. She said she couldn't recall ever seeing the Bible; however, she thought that is was around her home for a period of time.

    Sergeant Mohr got in touch with Mike Patten, the CPA of the Birmingham Gallery who stated that approximately four years ago he was at the McKinney household for dinner and during the course of the evening John McKinney showed him a large Bible of which McKinney said was a Guttenberg Bible. Mrs Patten also remembered John McKinney showing them the Bible. She said it was written in a foreign language and there were several colored prints or paintings within it.

    Sergeant Mohr then contacted Sally Saunders, former gallery partner of John McKinney who said that John McKinney

---

[209] Birmingham Police Department, Narrative Report, Sergeant Malcolm Mohr, December 12, 1977.

did have a Bible collection and she had heard that it was of great value. Sergeant Mohr thought that if John McKinney did have a Guttenberg Bible that this would be a motive for the homicide; however, Sergeant Mohr did not think that John McKinney possessed a Guttenberg Bible for the reason that a Bible of that age would not have colored plates within the book.[210]

Michigan State University Professor Clifton McChesney wrote a letter to Detectives Kalbfleisch and Sergeant Mohr regarding information he thought was important regarding the McKinney homicide.
He said Sally Saunders, former gallery partner of McKinney, was really shaken after seeing the murder scene — all the blood and the eye glasses on the floor. Then Saunders had described what she saw on McKinney's desk. McChesney wrote that Saunders described that the pendant McKinney had worn, and his watch, ring and wallet were stacked neatly on the table as though in preparation for a ritual. McChesney said that he had heard that McKinney also he had no shirt on when found. All of these things triggered memories for him.

      Clifton McChesney said that John McKinney and Doug Webster had visited his house when he had returned from a sabbatical from Japan in August of 1975. He thought that John's actions were peculiar when viewing his, McChesney's, artwork. He was viewing a painting, a blue triangle on a black field, and John had said as an aside, "You did have to paint that, didn't you?" He stated that McKinney and Webster were full of questions as to the

---

[210] Birmingham Police Dept., Narrative Report.

why, when and what of the painting. This was a piece for an upcoming exhibit.

They were both also very interested in Robert Knipchild's paintings of pyramids. Knipchild had exhibited in the gallery that fall. Doug Webster had said he was so interested in this concept that he had went to Ohio to visit Knipchild more than once. Apparently Knipchild and Webster had sat up all night talking about the power of pyramids.

John McKinney had told McChesney he had visited Clifford West's island off the coast of Georgia, which was a retreat for writers, musicians, poets, etc. He said he had a harmonic bond of minds with a woman writer there. McKinney stated he was very excited about this mental power and how they had communicated with few words.

After Clifton McChesney's exhibition in February of that year, he said John wanted to talk to him privately and told him that Doug Webster had planned on leaving the gallery to go to Arizona, because John's mind power was too great, and Doug could not take it anymore. John told him that he knew that people would think they were homosexual but this was not true. He explained that they had a relationship of power and that this was greater than a physical relationship.

Clifton said he and his wife talked at length about the information that John McKinney had divulged to him and what he had heard from Sally Saunders. The ritualistic stacking of material goods and the stripping of clothing sounded like something that happened in a ritualistic witchcraft sacrifice. He said the material he had read regarding these occult practices and the difference between white magic and black magic sounded as if John was to be penalized for something. McChesney said that even the calling card of leaving something and taking something that was of significant value spoke of this ritual. Perhaps referring to the artwork.

Sally Saunders was surprised that Marie of the Little Gallery had asked Sally if John was into witchcraft. Marie had told her that John had borrowed books on witchcraft from a gallery up north.

John had also told McChesney that he had an apartment, though no one he had talked with said they knew of this apartment.[211]

John McKinney had written a letter to Doug Webster in Arizona. The letter was dated March 22, 1977. He sent a check with the letter, stating both were way overdue. He said he was very happy for him in Arizona and wished him well at Yares Gallery. He also mentioned he was in a very heavy place and to try to write more about it would be wrong. He added he just needed a few days of sunshine and fresh air and would write more later.[212]

On April 12, 1977 Doug Webster wrote back to John McKinney. He stated that there was a troubling air about his note and couldn't put his finger on it exactly, but the same day he received the letter he was watching a news report and caught the story on the recent murders in Birmingham. And when they started showing pictures of the streets in Birmingham, and many people in it [the OCCK case] he got a terrible sinking feeling in the pit of his stomach about McKinney's letter. He stated that he had been uncomfortable about it ever since and he wished he would write and tell him what was happening in his life. Doug Webster felt that *John*

---

211 Clifton McChesney, Michigan State University, Letter to Sergeant Mohr and/or Lieutenant Kalbfleisch, October 1, 1977.
212 John McKinney, Letter to Doug Webster, March 22, 1977.

McKinney was being faced with some very critical decisions, the type that change a man's entire future.

Webster went to elaborate that his life continued to be one of incredible change. One that, he explained, so to speak, was an altering of atmospheres. And that even if he wanted to, he could not go backwards in time or space.

He told McKinney that even if there was distance between them, he would always be his friend.

He also wrote that the teachings of Don Juan were only those lessons that could be written down and the lessons he was experiencing he had no words for.[213]

Mysterious Art Connections

Two pieces of cloth art work were found in the center of John McKinney's desk the morning the body was found. Detectives Solomon and Mohr were trying to ascertain the source of the art work. No one at the gallery or associated with the gallery could advise where the art was from.[214] One piece of art was numbered or dated '76 and the other was numbered or dated '77.[215]

Regarding the batik done by an artist named Cigler, and signed Cigler '77, neither the Detroit Institute of Arts (DIA) nor Cranbrook Art Institute knew of this artist or work of art. These agencies were recommended to detectives by Mrs Joy Colby of *The Detroit News*.[216]

---

213 Doug Webster, Letter to John McKinney, April 12, 1977.
214 Birmingham Police Department, Narrative Report, Sergeant Mohr and Detective Solomon, September 26, 1977.
215 Interview of Lester Arwin, 3.
216 Birmingham Police Department, check on artist of batik.

The author, M.F. Cribari, of *Portraits in the Snow: The Oakland County Child Killings...Scandals and Small Conspiracies* was convinced that John McKinney was the child killer. She discussed the piece of art found on the desk of McKinney — that of a four-foot by five-foot cloth batik of a man. The batik was not framed and was signed Cigler. She noted that McKinney dealt mostly with local artists in his gallery and specialized in contemporary art, and yet a canvassing among the local art community by Birmingham detectives had failed to reveal who the artist was.[217]

Investigators also looked for a soft sculpture that was described as a series of ropes, arranged in a vertical pattern and colored red, blue and gold. This piece was pulled off a display wall the night McKinney was killed. Detectives thought that since there were many pieces of art that were much more expensive, the rope art had a $800 price tag, this particular piece might have been taken for some other reason. They were unsure of the particular reason.[218]

Detectives had not been able to find the piece in McKinney's files of artwork. Friends of McKinney mentioned to investigators that this was very unusual for him. He had been very meticulous man and was very good about logging in the art that came into his gallery.

M.F. Cribari communicated with an individual that was able to find out through a very reliable source that respectable art gallery owner/chaplain/husband and father led a double life. Perhaps even a triple life. That under the veneer of a loving, concerned citizen

---

[217] M.F. Cribari, *Portraits in the Snow: The Oakland County Child Killings...Scandals and Small Conspiracies*, (Denver: Outskirts Press, Inc., 2011), 285.
[218] Cribari, *Portraits in the Snow*, 286.

and art denizen there was bisexuality, illegal drugs and a host of dark and seedy friends. Allegedly he was quite the chameleon.[219]

Cribari also thought that the local authorities were encouraged to quickly wrap up the investigation through a few well-placed orders from on high. Without the big picture of the McKinney murder in hand, and the understanding that it was part of an even bigger picture, detectives were shunted from putting it together with the Oakland County Child Killer case. And they would have had to follow their orders. Perhaps some of them knew, or suspected, that this was part of a closely guarded case of some federal sort.[220]

Something that was to cause more than a few deaths regarding this investigation. Such as Berkley police officer Flynn, who managed to shoot himself twice in the chest. And it was ruled a suicide.

Cribari traced the McKinney murder back to the pedophile island of Francis Shelden, North Fox Island.[221] There was no way to communicate back then other than print or mail. It would have been a very valuable connection for those involved in the trafficking of children for sex, art, and films. Something that the connoisseur Dionysian crowd reveled in. It would have been a very valuable networked connection that McKinney provided, and it would have been provided with utmost confidence and security. Because perhaps those on high, such as Francis Shelden, never worried about getting caught like the bottom class criminals did, knowing that the feds had his back.

---

219 Ibid., 291.
220 Ibid., 293.
221 Ibid., 292.

But all of that ended with the pedophile North Fox Island ring being shut down when the arrest of all those who served the owner of the island and provided the patrons of the island going north and across the water wasn't possible anymore.

Whoever had designed the fantasy, Cribari believed, was one who believed that the tortuous murder of his subjects was a means to an end. It was the development and rendition of the sadistic art of his perfect "portraits."[222]

Certainly this significant fact applied to the sadistic portrait of a sketch of a boy who very much resembled Mark Stebbins, murder victim, screaming in pain and agony. This portrait hung on the wall in Christopher Busch's room.

Chrisopher Busch was a prime suspect in the OCCK case. And he most certainly wasn't an artist. Of course this wasn't found out until much later.

Then along came a gentleman named Patrick Coffey. It truly was a one in a million set of circumstance that revealed his set of revelations concerning the Christopher Busch debacle. He basically blew the lid right off of the case and risked his professional reputation and career by coming forward with the information he learned at the polygrapher's conference where he had met Larry Wasser who told him about "his suspect" he polygraphed that he thought was the OCCK.

Patrick Coffey sent M.F. Cribari copies of court documents showing Larry Wasser reversing all the allegations he had made concerning Christopher Busch. Rather than tell the truth of what Wasser had told Coffey, about the events which led Coffey to tell

---

222 Ibid., 294.

the King family about Christopher Busch, under oath Wasser recanted.[223]

According to Catherine King Broad, she had talked to Patrick Coffey about *Portraits in the Snow*. Patrick Coffey said John McKinney just happened to be a longtime family friend, and was over at their house all the time. The Coffey's were big time art collectors and their dad was business partners with McKinney. Tim King was also at the Coffey house all the time too, because he was friends with one of the Coffey boys, and Catherine King Broad was friends with one of the girls. John McKinney had eaten dinner many times over at their house. And for sure Timothy King would have been familiar with him and have gotten in a car with him. They all knew him as an art dealer, and they knew him as a reverend and he was known to have sometimes worn a clerical collar.

Catherine King Broad's childhood friend called her sister and told her about the allegations surrounding John McKinney. Her sister said it didn't surprise her. She said that around twelve years ago when she saw a news flash about a tip in the OCCK case, she felt compelled to write a letter to the authorities stating that they really needed to take a good look at McKinney. She felt he was totally creepy and that she had always suspected him. She then read *Portraits in the Snow*. Not knowing anything about the sex trafficking rings that were prevalent in the Detroit area and surrounding suburbs, she said that she had thought that John McKinney had did it and acted alone. She had nothing concrete to base it on, no evidence, but had carried this feeling with her for

---

223 Ibid., 307.

years and finally contacted the police. She said *he was a milquetoast and fastidious and scary.*²²⁴

---

224 Ibid., 308, 309.

Chapter 12

Business as Usual, the 70s and Serial Killers

Experts on ritual abuse state that pedophile rings are fronts for or extensions of hardcore Satanist cults. And it impossible to crack the command structure of cults if their illegal activities are not allowed to be pursued by the police or courts, which seems to be the case in many countries.[225]

Ted Gunderson, a former Los Angeles FBI official, warned about the spreading plague of Satanism and Satanic related crime. He sharply upbraided the bureau for covering up the crimes and the current crisis. He focused his strongest criticism on FBI Special Agent Kenneth Lanning, who was at the bureau's Behavioral Science unit at the FBI Training Academy in Quantico, Virginia.

The discovery of a Satanic burial site on an illegal drug plantation near Matamoros, Mexico, caused Lanning to go into hyperdrive denial. He penned a number of articles denying the existence of a Satanic problem in the United States, blaming the widespread concern over ritualistic crimes on religious fundamentalists, overzealous investigators, and quacks.

Lanning wrote in *Police Chief* magazine and in a special report distributed by the National Center for Missing and Exploited

---

[225] Mark Burdman, "Pedophiles arrested in Britain: 'More powerful than the Mafia,'" *Executive Intelligence Review* 16, no. 8 (1989): 43.

Children stating that more people have been killed in the names of Jesus and Mohammed than in the name of Satan.

"In my opinion, other than Aleister Crowley, Anton LaVey, and Michael Aquino, Ken Lanning is probably the most effective and foremost speaker for the Satanic movement in this country, today or any time in the past," said Ted Gunderson.[226]

Gunderson at one time had commanded 700 employees and an annual budget of $22.5 million, as the special agent in charge of the Los Angeles Field Division. When he retired in March of 1979, he set up a private firm, International Security Consultants (ISC).

One of the first investigations that Gunderson undertook with his private firm ISC was an investigation that involved a former Green Beret officer, Dr Jefferey McDonald, who was accused of murdering his wife and children in Fayetteville, North Carolina in 1970. Jeffery McDonald contends that his family was murdered by a Satanic cult similar to the Manson Family, which were active on the West Coast and had carried out their cultic murders just months before his family was murdered.

While working with the attorneys representing Dr McDonald, Gunderson became increasingly aware of the existence of a nationwide Satanic underworld engaged in drug trafficking, pornography, ritualistic murders, and other crimes. Gunderson then developed an expertise in the field.

Ted Gunderson was instrumental in investigating the alleged ritualistic sexual abuse of children in the McMartin Day School,

---

226 Ted Gunderson Interview, "FBI's Lanning sides with Satan, says former top bureau official," *Executive Intelligence Review* 17, no. 23 (1990): 66.

and in helping to develop that case. Then in 1983 with investigative journalist Maury Terry, the author of *The Ultimate Evil*, a book concerning the Son of Sam case, he helped to develop critical evidence demonstrating the ritualistic murder of Broadway impresario Roy Radin.

Based on his experiences investigating the McDonald murders, the McMartin case, and other murders, Ted Gunderson contends that a nationwide Satanic underground exists in the United States. He said the investigations he had conducted over a 10-year period led him to the exact opposite conclusion that Ken Lanning described.[227]

"There is every indication that there is a loose-knit Satanic cult network operating in the US." said Gunderson. He described it as a combination of a high-level group of people linked to child pornography, prostitution, drug trafficking and other criminal activity internationally. Then this top level organized structure filtered down to independent groups of Satanists most likely not tied to the first network. He said the local groups also engage in drug trafficking and ritualistic activities like animal and human sacrifices. Below these groups Gunderson said that he and fellow investigators encountered high school age kids who go to the occult shops and buy the Satanic literature and set up their own independent groups.

"From hundreds of interviews that I have personally conducted in every part of the country, I encounter a persistent pattern everywhere. All the stories fit the same mold: animal and baby sacrifices, the use of candles and other ritualistic props, robes,

---

227 Gunderson, "FBI's Lanning," 67.

chanting etc. All of these victim-survivors, from children to adults, are telling the same basic story." Gunderson said.

Ted Gunderson cited his investigation in the McDonald case as evidence against various players in the system covering up the Satanic crimes. He stated he had obtained a signed affidavit from Helene Stokely, a member of the Satanic cult that carried out the murders of the McDonald family. A prosecutor ignored that evidence and proceeded to prosecute Dr McDonald for murdering his family.

"I have evidence chiseled in stone showing that the U.S. Army and the Department of Justice covered up that Satanic angle and framed up Dr McDonald. Why? Among other things the McDonald case could have exposed a major heroin-smuggling operation out of Vietnam involving highly placed Army officials running drugs into the US in the body cavities of dead American GIs—green body bags loaded with heroin...But that was just the tip of the iceberg." Gunderson said.

Gunderson felt that a federal clearing house for intelligence on Satanic-related crime should be created. He pointed the finger at the FBI in thwarting efforts for progress in this regard stating that the FBI was consciously attempting to bury the entire issue and drive local police into dropping their own efforts into investigating those types of crimes. "I am convinced that we are confronted with a serious Satanic penetration of every level of society and government at every level." He said.[228]

It was the black magician Aleister Crowley who was at the forefront of laying the occult foundations in the United States. During WWI,

---

228 Ibid.

Crowley entered the US in 1916 as the head of an OTO lodge, spreading its influence and teachings. Then later during WWII, Crowley helped to establish an OTO lodge in Pasadena, California. Subsequent OTO branches popped up in a number of US cities, including New York and Houston. So in effect a loose network was around and already functioning via the occult shops and bookstores; which included newsletters, ads in the underground press, and other methods — before the Process Church arrived in 1967.[229]

Traumatic abuse creates dissociative states in children and is one of the reasons that the CIA and other intelligence agencies have played key roles in the creation of relatively mainstream Satanic groups while also denying the existence of and covering up underground Satanic cults engaged in violent criminal activities. Evidence suggests that a multitude of Satanic groups have served as intelligence "fronts" for mind control operations.[230]

In lock step with the rampage of killings taking place, the FBI's Behavioral Sciences came of age in the mid-1970s. The new "science" of criminal profiling was created along with the new term "the serial killer." The national lexicon was forever changed and a burgeoning industry of these types of killers seemed to grow with it, with the new mass murderer becoming a type of anti-hero. The public was given a full course gore driven meal via the media, who created larger than life figures out of these criminals: Henry Lee Lucas, David Berkowitz, Theodore Bundy, John Wayne Gacy, and

---

[229] Maury Terry, *The Ultimate Evil*, (New York: Barnes and Noble, 1987), 180,181.
[230] David McGowan, *Programmed to Kill: The Politics of Serial Murder*, (NY: iUniverse, 2004), xviii.

Angelo and Kenneth Bianchi, who were collectively known as the "Hillside Stranglers."[231]

Henry Lee Lucas, probably having the longest run of the killers, disclosed his story to a writer, who wrote *The Hand of Death: The Henry Lee Lucas Story*. The book details Lucas's indoctrination into a nationwide Satanic cult. Lucas said he was trained by this cult in a mobile paramilitary training camp in the Florida Everglades. His training included instruction in abduction and arson techniques, as well as in the fine art of killing someone up close and personal. Apparently his instructors were so impressed with his handling of a knife that they allowed him to teach others his techniques in the cult. Lucas stated he served this cult in various ways, including as a contract killer and as an abductor of children, whom he delivered to a ranch in Mexico near Juarez (sounding very similar to the CIA Finder's operation). Once the children were delivered to the ranch, they were used in the production of child pornography and used in ritual sacrifices. Lucas said the cult's base of operations was based in Texas; included trafficking in children and drugs and other illegal endeavors.[232]

It was on June 30, 1998, that Henry Lee Lucas was scheduled for execution in the state of Texas. His total number of victims ranged from 300 to 600, and although numbers were likely inflated, he had savagely murdered many victims of various ages, races and genders, having no particular preference. It looked as though the execution of Lucas would proceed as planned. Then a most remarkable thing happened. Twelve days before the scheduled date Governor George H. Bush made a special request that the

---

231 Ibid., 163.
232 Ibid., 73, 74.

Texas State Board of Pardons and Paroles, all Bush appointees, review Lucas's case. Then very uncharacteristic of this Board, members recommended that the execution not take place. The Board stated that there was a possibility that Henry Lee Lucas was in fact innocent, and wasn't a serial killer after all.[233]

Henry Lee Lucas had explicitly stated that the cult included among its members various socially prominent individuals, and included high-level politicians. Perhaps the reason for the pardon by Texas Governor George H Bush.[234]

In 1976 three mass murder cases plagued the administration of Jimmy Carter and Walter Mondale, and to a great degree shaped the modus operandi of many organized and semi-organized sex trafficking and pedophile rings. The serial murder cases — Son of Sam, the Jonestown Massacre, and the Atlanta murders not only demonstrated they were not isolated phenomenon, but linked to a network of cults operating in the United States.

The Son of Sam murders began in the summer of 1977, murdering or seriously maiming 13 young white men and women in New York City. These serial murders were the work of a Satanic, Aleister Crowley worshipping cult developed by psychiatrists out of a drug running clique operating in Westchester, New York and in North Dakota. According to investigator Maury Terry, David Berkowitz had identified a 20-member ring of drug users that deployed him and others for the Son of Sam killings. Over the period of several years, the members of the ring were molded psychiatrically, or mind controlled, through a process involving

---

233 Ibid., 71, 72.
234 Ibid., 76.

LSD use and ritualistic animal mutations, into a Satanic cult capable of conducting the ritualistic mass-terror murders.[235]

While independent law enforcement and investigative journalists described how a Satanic cult was at the center of the Son of Sam murders and that there was more than one killer, some powerful individuals and institutions enforced the cover-up that the murders were the work of one killer, David Berkowitz. To aid in this narrative of a lone assassin being solely responsible, Berkowitz was never brought to trial.

Investigator Maury Terry then found evidence which linked the Son of Sam cult to the Process Church, (a Satanic church linked to Charles Manson), which was founded in London in the 1960s and then established itself in the United States.

Investigators discovered that an attorney, John Markham, was intimately involved with the leadership of the Process Church.

According to a source who was a member, the Son of Sam cult intersected with numerous other Satanic cults in the New York metropolitan area. The same source also stated that the Son of Sam cult had its East Coast headquarters in an abandoned church in Westchester County, New York, near the Putnam County line, and that members frequented a number of estates within that area.

A man named Christopher Fripp, who was a leading member of the Process Church, owned an estate in the Westchester town of Pound Ridge, the very area described by Maury Terry's source. And according to a researcher who had infiltrated the

---

[235] Ira Liebowitz, "The child pornography lobby protects cults, drugs, and mass murder," *Executive Intelligence Review* 10, no. 49 (1983): 29.

Process Church, the Pound Ridge estate was used secretly by the upper echelon members of the Church.[236]

An informant named Vinny also said that there were affluent people associated with the Son of Sam cult. There were many facts that supported Vinny's claim. When David Berkowitz was arrested, he possessed a list of telephone numbers which according to Maury Terry, were barely investigated by the NYPD. Terry enlisted sources in the telephone company to identify the names behind the mysterious telephone numbers.

One number was identified as that of an exclusive country club in Long Island's Hamptons area, the Montauk Gold and Racquet Club. Two other numbers were listed as summer residences of Yonkers New York doctors. They were not office numbers.

Another number was that of a private residence in East Hampton, and another belonged to an unlisted telephone in West Babylon, Long Island. A final number was listed to a private home on exclusive Shelter Island, Long Island.

There really was no legitimate reason, according to Maury Terry, for Yonkers, New York, postal clerk David Berkowitz to possess these particular telephone numbers. He also didn't list any identifying names next to the numbers.[237]

Almost as soon as the murders stopped with the arrest of David Berkowitz for the Son of Sam Murders, the Jonestown murders occurred.

---

236 EIR Investigative Team, "New evidence links CAN 'cult awareness; network to satanists," *Executive Intelligence Review* 18, no.32 (1991): 67.
237 Terry, *Ultimate Evil*, 379.

There was a series of public scandals in San Francisco in 1977 over child abuse occurring in Jim Jones's cult. The cult then fled to Guyana where Jones ordered the mass-murder and suicides of 913 of his mainly black followers. Allegedly the mass murders were triggered by Tim Stoen, a cult defector who exposed the child abuse. Stoen, a cult member and assistant District Attorney in San Francisco, worked with cult attorney Eugene Chaitkin to help organize Jones's first major financial scam. Stoen and Chaitkin had set up an extensive operation where the cult obtained court-awarded guardianship of hundreds of children (both children of cult members and homeless children) in order to secure for Jones welfare, social security, and child support monies. The swindle ultimately resulted in the murder of 276 children in Guyana, nearly half of them court awarded children.

The Jones People's Temple Cult had originally been created and sponsored by five very prominent religious figures working with the Eli Lilly Foundation in Indianapolis, Indiana. These religious figures were New York Episcopalian Bishop Paul Moore, who was affiliated with St. John the Divine Cathedral, Rabbi Maurice Davis of White Plains, New York; Rabbi Murray Salzman of the Baltimore Hebrew Congregation and the U.S. Commission on Civil Rights; Bishop James Armstrong, chairman of the National Council of Churches, and Monsignor Raymond T. Bosler of the Indianapolis Catholic Archdiocese Communications Division.

After the devastation of the Jones cult, a series of murders involving black children began in Atlanta, Georgia. The children were asphyxiated and mutilated. The murders stopped in 1981 with the arrest and conviction of Wayne Williams. The serial murder spree claimed the lives of at least 29 children. The arrest of Wayne

Williams was shortly after the intervention of Roy Innis, the Congress of Racial Equality national chairman. He brought forth a witness who was able to name names of members of a Satanic group that had evolved out of a Miami and Atlanta drug-trafficking ring that used young children as runners in Atlanta. The ring became involved in child pornography and child prostitution and performed ritual murders within the ring and with other children. Wayne Williams was the ring's recruiter and photographer.

    Detailed information provided by a witness was covered up. The information was given to FBI special agent for Atlanta John Glover and Atlanta Police Commissioner Lee Brown. Investigators believe that a decision was made at some level to temporarily halt the serial cultic murders with the arrest of Wayne Williams. According to several sources, the cultic murder ring's clientele in drugs, child pornography, and prostitution involved some of the highest-ranking members of Atlanta's political establishment.[238]

Noreen Gosch, mother of kidnapped boy, Johnny Gosch, knew her son's kidnapping was not a random act, but one of an organized pedophile ring. The pedophile rings were international in scope and they had auctions of children for buyers. The auctions would take place all over the country, and operators would constantly move them to different locations so they wouldn't be detected. FBI agent Ted Gunderson had multiple verifications of the existence of such auctions and said that they took place in most major cities of the US. Noreen Gosch learned from victim Paul Bonacci that it was Lieutenant Colonel Michael Aquino who had purchased Johnny

---

238 Liebowitz, "Child Porn Lobby," 29.

directly from his kidnappers within two weeks after he was taken.[239]

According to Johnny Gosch and at least three other people, it was Michael Aquino who picked him up and paid for him in Sioux City, Iowa, after he was kidnapped. Referred to as "the Colonel," reports have Michael Aquino connected not only to the abduction of Johnny Gosch, but other high profile abduction cases of boys, such as Eugene Martin, and Jacob Wetterling. There were other abductions of boys in the Midwest also.

The boys were chosen and then kidnapped to create a perfect mind control slave to use for blackmail and murder purposes; whatever their "owners" required. To accomplish this they had to be subjected to Satanic programming which created MPD or DID (Multiple Personality Disorder or Dissociate Identity Disorder) which produced a series of personalities suited to a variety of assignments from the associated controllers.

Michael Aquino worked in the field of military intelligence. During the time of Johnny Gosch's kidnapping, he was with the Defense Intelligence Agency and attended the Foreign Service Institute at the Department of State. He was in Washington D.C. from 1981 through 1984. According to Cathy O'Brien, (a mind controlled presidential model, sex slave and courier) Aquino regularly attended White House functions and palled around with George Bush and Dick Cheney.

The record shows that he was in military service during the time of the kidnapping. He was then a major writing "From Psyops

---

239 Noreen N. Gosch, *Why Johnny Can't Come Home*, (West Des Moines: The Johnny Gosch Foundation, 2000), 105-7.

to Mindwar," describing mind control techniques and their use in the military.[240]

Mark Phillips, Cathy O'Brien's husband and rescuer from the Monarch Mind Control Program, stated that the revised Monarch Project was under the direction of U.S. Army Major (who would eventually become a Colonel) Michael Aquino, who would put a new twist on the program and add Satanism to the mix.

According to Phillips, the Defense Intelligence Agency is a politically governed/operated US government intelligence gathering agency whose responsibilities, progress, and assignments are "monitored" by the intelligence committees of both the House and Senate. He said that this equated to politicians having access to ultra secret, ultra dangerous information which they can, and have used, against innocent US citizens for their perverse pleasure and profits. Totally undetected.[241]

The Franklin Cover-up was an investigation led by John De Camp, and involved many mind control assets and high-end government officials involved in Satanism, drugs, pedophile rings, sex trafficking and the making of child pornography and snuff films. The initial investigation concerned the Franklin Credit Union and laundered money, but which then turned out to be a whole lot more than a simple investigation of a mismanaged savings and loan. At the end of the investigation there would be evidence of money laundering via the Iran/Contra scandal and the involvement of the North American Man/Boy Love Association (NAMBLA), which

---

240 Ibid., 223.
241 Ibid., 240, 241.

put five million in the Franklin Credit Union as a nonprofit called the "Church of the Beloved Disciple."[242]

NAMBLA also figured prominently in the case of North Fox Island owner and pedophile, Francis Shelden, along with his *Spartacus* publication writer and editor friend, John Stamford. The organization was formed in 1978, and head of NAMBLA, Peter Thorstad, saw the organization grow from a $600 in the bank small affair with a handful of subscribers to a multimillion-dollar organization.

Psychiatrist Dr Judy Ann Densen exposed the organization's agenda that its members believe that they have a constitutional right to have sex with children. She was then branded public enemy number one by NAMBLA.

Paul Bonacci, mind control victim, personally heard Peter Thorstad say of Judi-Ann Densen Gerber, "I'm going to have to get rid of that bitch." One of the attributes of mind control is that victims often possess a photographic memory and are able to remember the tiniest of details most people would forget. Paul Bonacci had a photographic memory and could remember every person he had been with and describe it in detail.

Bonacci also stated that he went to Washington D.C., to have sex with U.S. Representative Barney Frank. He also traveled to New York to become a "boytoy" for the head of NAMBLA, Peter Thorstad — and one of Bonacci's dissociated personality alters was created and based on Thorstad's specifications.

On national TV Peter Thorstad was asked by a host of the ABC talk show, *The Last Word*, if a boy as young as nine could give

---

242 Ibid., 113.

consent to have sex with a man. "Of course!," he said, "They do it all the time!"[243]

The main photographer of the pornography and snuff films involved in the Franklin scandal was a man named Rusty Nelson.[244] He worked with Lawrence King, who was the manager of the Franklin Federal Credit Union, and a rising star in state and national Republican circles. King was an officer in the National Black Republican Council and sang the national anthem at the GOP national convention in 1984 and in 1988.[245]

Lawrence King was also connected to Craig Spence, who among other things, dabbled in child kidnapping to supply the needs of his many customers of his call boy ring, which included the CIA's MK Ultra Monarch project.

Photographer Russell (Rusty) Nelson was a central figure in the Franklin Scandal. He had in his possession large amounts of physical evidence, including photographs, that implicated prominent law enforcement and political figures in crimes of child abuse, child pornography and kidnapping, drug smuggling, money laundering, and illegal campaign financing. The case was tied to the Iran/Contra drugs for arms affair and also tied to illegal activities of the FBI and CIA.[246]

Rusty Nelson stated that he was a private photographer for Larry King, and his duties included taking secret photos of specific people, if they "got together." Nelson said that he not only took

---

243 Ibid., 209, 210.
244 Ibid., 151.
245 John W. DeCamp, *The Franklin Cover-Up: Child Abuse, Satanism, and Murder in Nebraska*, (2nd ed. Lincoln: AWT Inc., 1996), xxi.
246 Gosch, *Johnny*, 151, 152.

pictures for King, but secretly kept identical copies of this same film which he mailed to his place of residence. He also said that he took audiotapes, computer disks, and paper copies of documents, including ledgers, without Larry King's knowledge. Nelson said he retained these documents and extra film he mailed to himself for insurance so that he stayed alive. He said that at one time Lawrence King "flat out told me" that he had a man killed to look like a suicide.

It was Rusty Nelson who gave the photographs and other documents he procured to investigator Gary Caradori on July 11, 1990, the day of Caradori's fatal flight from Chicago, which killed Caradori and his eight-year old son, A.J. Caradori had called Senator Loren Schmit, who was working on the Franklin Scandal at the time, that he had the smoking gun evidence as to who was involved, and would fly home that night. Except he never made it home, his plane exploded in mid-air. The wreckage was strewn over nearly a mile wide area of a cornfield, near the town of Aurora, Illinois. A farmer said he had seen a fireball then heard an explosion.

A sheriff's deputy at the crash site began picking up photographs that were given to Gary Caradori by Rusty Nelson. They were of recognizable politicians with children, and it was reported that there were "porn pictures scattered in the field." The deputy stated that the FBI snatched the photos from his hands, told him to leave and told him to keep his mouth shut. The deputy left but didn't keep his mouth shut. Less than a year later he was severely injured in a car crash that killed his wife and he can no longer work.[247]

---

247 Ibid., 154, 155.

Sandie Caradori never received official notification of her husband's and son's deaths. She heard the news from friends who had heard it on the radio. And early the next day after their deaths, before their bodies were sent home from Illinois, the FBI descended on Caradori's office with a subpoena for all of his records.

Loren Schmit confirmed that Gary Caradori had been trying to obtain photographs that some alleged victims said were taken of them during the period when they were abused. He also confirmed that Caradori had been told that some of those victims were allegedly involved in child sexual abuse involving Satanic cults and Caradori was working on the places and times regarding this abuse. He was also working on the leads into Washington, D.C.[248]

The wreckage of Gary Caradori's plane was taken to and examined on a military base rather than at a location under the control of civilian personnel. The crash was then ruled an "accident" by government officials and not an act of sabotage.[249]

---

248 DeCamp, *Franklin*, 3.
249 Gosch, *Johnny*, 155.

Chapter 13

The OCCK as Occult Ritual

It was 1976. America had just celebrated its Bicentennial birthday. The Vietnam War had ended a year before and there was a feeling of hope throughout the country. It was as if waking from a bad geopolitical nightmare and the country could begin again anew. The Detroit airwaves were floating in the sound frequencies of Stevie Wonder and Marvin Gaye, and all was right with the world.

Then came the kid killer near Detroit.

There are many indications that the entire series of killings of the OCCK were orchestrated as an occult ritual. The ritual was designed to be carried on the frequency wave of a certain current and projected into the future.

Most of the occult details have been covered up by those that managed the case. And the FBI.

There is a realm of activity that includes secrecy, false identities, clandestine murder and other curious circumstances by which the general population is entertained but usually remains oblivious to its presence — Espionage.[250]

---

250 Walter Bosley and Richard B. Spence, *Empire of the Wheel: Espionage, Murder and the Occult in Southern California* (California: Corvos Books, 2011), Loc 2935, Kindle Edition.

Part of this hidden warfare and espionage included occult workings. Aleister Crowley was a master magician and came quite early into this scene to set up and start various occult "workings."

In fact, it was William Melville of Scotland Yard's Special Branch who had recruited Sidney Reilly (Schlomo Rosenblum), also called the Ace of Spies, and Aleister Crowley, for missions abroad.

The assignment and wartime mission to America for Crowley was arranged and overseen by his friend, Everard Feilding, who was also secretary of the London Society for Psychical Research and a veteran investigator of mediumistic phenomena.[251]

Crowley's first stop was Detroit. He went to Parke-Davis, the pharmaceutical company, and picked up refined peyote (mescalin) to use ritually as he had before in practicing the rites of Eleusis, the rites which were associated with the San Bernadino working in California.[252]

James Sheldby Downard described an America imbued with "Masonic Sorcery" and "call to chaos" cultism and "mystical toponomy" — an America where in which literally nothing was as it seemed.[253]

Was 1976, a premier slice of time and space on the American landscape, a part of this occult working? Were there clues that this could be the case?

There was an individual who may have been part of the ritual killing. William H. McGill was killed on the night of July 3,

---

[251] Bosley and Spence, *Empire*, Loc 2289.
[252] Ibid., Loc 2934.
[253] Ibid., Loc 1676.

1976, or in the early morning of July 4, 1976, in his apartment in Detroit. He was found to have six separate and distinct fires set around his body. There were also tattoos on his body, one of which was the "Goat of Mendez."[254]

The fires and a red candle at the murder scene led investigators to believe that this was a ritual killing. Mr McGill was a known homosexual. Was McGill a stand in for Osiris, the Egyptian God of death and then rebirth? The fire ritual of the god involved priests gathering before dawn at the god's shrine to re-enact the first appearance of the sun by lighting a fire in a brazier.[255]

Detectives questioned Wayne Forest West, a onetime OCCK suspect before he disappeared, as to the death of William McGill. Mr West was quite the occult adept and well known around town, having many articles written about him and his doings in the Church of Satan and his other occult activities.

William McGill had been stabbed over 114 times.

Detectives showed West a photo of McGill and he said he didn't know who he was and had never seen him. The name McGill didn't ring a bell either with West. Apparently McGill had been involved with the Church of Satan but West couldn't remember his face. Or his name.

"...but so many of the people in that organization at the time, I mean, I couldn't tell you what their real names were anyway,

---

[254] Detroit Police Department, Detectives Bone and Turney, Wayne Forest West Interview, 3:00 pm, April 18, 1977.
[255] Joshua J. Mark, "Clergy, Priests & Priestesses in Ancient Egypt," March 7, 2017, World History Encyclopedia, https://www.worldhistory.org/article/1026/clergy-priests—priestesses-in-ancient-egypt/.

because they all used alias's and pseudonyms, and so on and so forth. I guess I was the only person that publicly broadcast myself. Neither his face, nor, nor the name ring a bell to me." said West.

Detectives rattled off a list of names that West might have known. Nothing. Then they got to a name…

"Wonder if the last name of Thibideau—?"

"Thibideau---" said West.

The name caused quite a reaction from West's attorney, Mr Hand.

"Ask him if we could [redacted] interview. Right now." said Hand.

West then countered the attorney's reaction.

"That rings a bell someplace too, but again I can't place the individual, but the name rings a bell." said West.

Wayne Forest West did recognize the Goat of Mendez tattoo though.[256]

James Shelby Downard coined the term Masonic Sorcery theatre to describe a ritual that would be known to occult initiates if they came across its evidence, but was unknown to everyone else. In this scenario, the time, the place and many of the victim's details of death might have been arranged according to the ritual purposes of the perpetrators and the ritual indicators would be all but invisible to the uninitiated.[257]

Aleister Crowley's magickal Amalantrah Working took place in Montauk, New York between January 14 and 16, 1918. Crowley

---

[256] Bone and Turney, West Interview.
[257] Bosley and Spence, *Empire*, Loc 2481.

mentions Montauk in his diaries on June 20, 1918. He said the magickal retirement made it clear the current was exhausted...Perhaps finished or exhausted in his end of the working and then signaling to others in Detroit they could then pick up the current.[258]

Going back in time to Detroit, Crowley's spiritual son there was used in helping with the Amalantrah working in that area. Was this magikal working for priming the pump for the war effort based in Detroit? The weapons manufacturing at *Campus Martius*?[259]

Charles Stanfield Jones was Crowley's star pupil, and magickal heir. Jones was taken under Crowley's wing and on March 30, 1918, Jones sold all his possessions and boarded a train from Vancouver to New York to join Crowley in the Great Work. Jones adopted the magical motto Arctaeon, which was given to him by the wizard Amalantrah in a series of ecstatic magickal workings that Crowley was conducting at the time. Jones's revelation concerning *The Book of the Law*, summarized in his essay "Liber 31," convinced Crowley that Jones was his "magical son."[260]

Master Illusionist and escapologist Harry Houdini had also visited Aleister Crowley's recruiter, William Melville of Scotland Yard's Special Branch.[261] Houdini had attracted the bitter hatred of the spiritualists, mediums and communities that he worked to defame and uncover as liars and charlatans. It was in Montreal, Canada where the suspected spiritualist agent, Joscelyn Gordon Whitehead,

---

258 Ibid., Loc 2750-2759.
259 Ibid., Loc 2750.
260 Richard Kaczynski, *Panic in Detroit*, (New York: Sekhmet Books, 2015), 5.
261 Bosley and Spence, *Empire*, Loc 2289.

punched Houdini in the gut, damaging his already possibly poisoned appendix, though Houdini would actually die in Detroit. Both locales occupy important points in the telluric (energetic Earth) grid.[262] This knowledge is often used in magickal purposes, for good or ill.

One of the earliest references to Earth energy grids or leys was documented by Dr John Dee, the Royal astrologer and magician to Queen Elizabeth I.

The true mathematical science is that which measureth the invisible lines and immortal beams which can pass through cold and turf, hill and dale. It was for this reason, it was accounted by all ancient priests the chiefest science; for it gave them power both in their words and works.[263]

John Dee was one of the founders of modern Scottish Rite Freemasonry.

This knowledge of Earth energies, or leys, was secretly known to a select few in every human organization throughout the world, and its use transcended all societies groups and religions. In California leys were used by the Catholic Church, and the church and its supposed nemesis, Freemasonry, cooperated in their secret use. It appeared that an esoteric stream flowed through all human activity, supplying the initiating energy for apparently random and unrelated events on the surface of history. The stream didn't belong to one

---

262 Ibid., Loc 2812.
263 Maria Wheatley, *Divining Ancient Sites: Insights into their creation*, (Marlborough: Celestial Songs Press, 2014), 17.

secret society, religion or group, nor could it —because it was the very fabric of reality itself.[264]

There is evidence that the ancients had an advanced knowledge of both mind and matter and understood how these two aspects of reality were related to each other. The gravitational system of the ley lines were an integral tool of this known technology, or to use a term coined by Russian researchers— psychotronics.[265]

The practice of "sacrifice to the gods" came from this ancient knowledge of leys where the killing of a person or animal upon a megalith or stone acted as a kind of "primer" to stimulate the flow of its energy. The original practice of a sacrifice would have been an exact science performed by a priest or priestess who had great knowledge of how to obtain the greatest effects from such an endeavor. It would have involved carrying out the sacrifice in a particular way and at specific times determined by the positions of astronomical bodies. When the ancient advanced civilizations collapsed, sacrifice continued together with its relationship to ley lines.

The exact mechanism of how a sacrifice works in a materialistic sense is unclear. The vital energy flowing out of and collecting at a ley in some way is attracted to the vital energy that is poured out and into it in the form of a sacrifice. The sacrifice then functions as an action "primer;" it stimulates the system and sets it into operation. In some way the sacrifice "psychically charges" the ley in a way that is similar to the way an electrical condenser is

---

[264] Sesh Heri, *The Handprint of Atlas*, (Highland, CA: Corvos Books, 2010), 54.
[265] Heri, *Atlas*, 135.

charged with electricity. Another method of this type of "psychic" charging is the burial of people, animals, plants or personal artifacts at the site of a ley.[266]

Theoretically this energy can be released as desired by inserting a smaller amount of energy into a relevant center stone, as circle stones have bands of alternating charge, usually seven, and the energy is derived from the center of the circle and transmitted concentrically outward, to be stored in the perimeter after the magickal working is accomplished.[267]

The Rosicrucian magi of the Renaissance referred to the psychometric function of leys as "memory theatre."

It is the conventional assumption that statues and other architectural features only have an aesthetic or symbolic quality associated with them. Yet it appears that the great architects have secretly known that objects such as statues, obelisks, and other architectural artifices are susceptible to psychic charging, and susceptible to being imbued with the memory of events both in the past and the future.[268]

The route that Aleister Crowley took on his trip to the west coast of the United States in 1915, as identified by author and investigator Sesh Heri, was a virtual tour of a planetary energy line system using geomorphological principles.[269]

Ley lines are what are considered tools in what the Freemasons call "the Great Work," the development of humanity into a higher form of being, which was the alchemical quest of the ages to transform the "lead" of ordinary human consciousness into

---

266 Ibid., 136.
267 Bosley and Spence, *Empire*, Loc 2926.
268 Heri, *Atlas*, 49.
269 Bosley and Spence, *Empire*, Loc 2919.

the "gold" of super-consciousness. This work seems to have followed the trajectory of two paths. One aimed at the spiritual and physical elevation of all individuals through the principle of seeding important ideas relating to this concept and having them multiply; while another path aimed at exploiting the masses and the "shearing of their golden fleece," or their latent psychic powers, which are then consumed and utilized by an exploitative and magical elite. The two pathed agenda of this alchemical quest appears to run throughout history as an on-going and secret magical war between the forces of light and dark and good and evil, and out of this ongoing conflict emerges what we call "history."[270]

OCCK investigators came across information relating to Zain or Zayin, the Aeon of Horus and the writings of Aleister Crowley.[271] They then visited the Emmanuel Temple to decipher the Hebrew and the Rabbi informed them that Zayin is the seventh letter of the Hebrew alphabet.[272]

Wayne Forest West had converted to Judaism. And was studying Hebrew.

Detectives noted that Tim King's body was found on Gill Road, and that it could possibly be related to the murder of William McGill.[273] A beginning, an ending, and a new beginning perhaps. Ushering in the Aeon of Horus, son of the slain Osiris. A gill is also related to a fish. And the symbolism is pertinent to Christianity.

---

270 Heri, *Atlas*, 142.
271 Special Assignment, Timothy King Homicide, Detective Notes.
272 Special Assignment, King Homicide.
273 Ibid.

The beginnings of a ritualistic aspect to the OCCK murders was sketched out by investigators. Investigators noted the dates on which the victims were held, the holidays, and the length of time they were held. Astrological data was also noted for each victim.[274]

Particular evidence was certainly indicative of a ritual being involved. The way the victims were cleaned. There could have been painting on the bodies, and then they were cleansed. The way they were cared for. Detectives noted that it could have all been planned. And ordered to specification.[275]

The main action took place on Woodward Avenue, also known as M1. This was the original highway called "Detroit Main Street." It was one of five principal avenues along with Michigan, Grand River, Gratiot and Jefferson. Woodward Avenue was synonymous with Detroit, cruising culture, and the automotive industry. Woodward Avenue followed the route of the old Saginaw Trail, which was an Indian trail that connected to the Mackinaw Trail.

Woodward Avenue had the distinction of being the location of the first mile of concrete paved roadway in the country. Industrialists needed a system of roads, along with the cars manufactured in Detroit, to run the combined oil/energy system. Along with the 1913 Federal Reserve banking cartel, the State Trunkline Highway System was created in Michigan, with WWI following shortly thereafter in 1914.

Woodward Avenue starts as an intersection with Jefferson Avenue next to Hart Plaza, about 750 feet from the Detroit River. Hart Plaza is regarded as the birthplace of the Ford Motor

---
274 Ibid.
275 Ibid.

Company, and is located near Cobo Center and the Renaissance Center.[276]

Woodward Avenue was named after the original city designer of Detroit, the Freemason Augustus Woodward. The most prominent streets which were part of the original gridwork of Woodward's city layout were those listed previously: Woodward, Michigan, Gratiot, Grand River and Jefferson Avenues.

Augustus Woodward was good friends with President Jefferson, and part of his intimate circle. Jefferson appointed him as Michigan's first Chief Justice in 1805.[277]

The four cities that the four victims of the OCCK lived in were situated right off of Woodward Avenue. The abductions followed a trajectory of moving north along Woodward Avenue. The first victim, Mark Stebbins, lived in Ferndale, the city closest to Detroit. He was abducted February 15, 1976. The second victim, Jill Robinson, lived in Royal Oak, a city north of Ferndale. She was abducted December 22, 1976. The third victim, Kristine Mihelich, lived in Berkley, a city north of Royal Oak. She was abducted January 2, 1977. The fourth victim, Timothy King, lived in Birmingham, a city north of Berkley. He was abducted March 16, 1977.

Were the abductions considered part of the ley line system? According to author and investigator Sesh Heri, Detroit sits on one of the two main spirals of telluric power in the United States, the other spiral is located in San Diego, California. Heri maintains that

---

276 Wikipedia, M-1 (Michigan highway), https://en.wikipedia.org/wiki/M-1_(Michigan_highway).
277 Chad Stuemke, "Stargate Detroit," *Chad Stuemke: Ancient Sacred Landscapes, Hidden Archeology and Modern Mystical Cities.* https://chadstuemke.com/stargate-detroit-i/.

these spirals emanate very powerful energy. The energy flow through the described area is stronger than the energy flow through a single line far away from the spirals.[278] Thus, any magic performed in Detroit would theoretically have greater impact than the areas off of the spiral.

It is further theorized that when Aleister Crowley was in Detroit doing magickal workings it might have front loaded whatever he did when he went to Chicago to meet up with a variety of espionage contacts.[279] The same idea or theory could be also be applied to the child murders of the OCCK along Woodward Avenue.

Then there was the strange phenomenon of no one knowing the name of the batik artist whose artwork was displayed prominently across murder victim John McKinney's desk. In an art town where all the artists knew each other and each other's art works, constantly mingling in galleries and shows, this would be unheard of.

The artist was most likely Dennis Cigler. According to his resume, his work was inspired by ancient history, classical culture and its myths. He also had some private showings in the Detroit area. There was a showing for scenery and costumes in batik for Bizet's *The Pearl Fishers* production at the Michigan Opera. The production of *The Pearl Fishers* by the Michigan Opera Theatre began in 1978 through 1979. Another showing was organized for the Theatre Company in Detroit in September 1978. And the final listing on the resume of Cigler was for a showing at the Grosse

---

278 Bosley and Spence, *Empire*, Loc 2933.
279 Ibid., Loc 2943.

Point War Memorial in September of 1978.[280] The War Memorial was once Russell A. Alger's house, a relative of Frances Shelden, the millionaire owning North Fox Island and accused of running an international pedophile ring.

Later on art and architecture would be constructed in Hart Plaza, sitting at the base of GM's headquarters and Woodward Avenue. According to occult researchers, the artwork is endowed with what has been termed, "stargate" symbolism. Which according to mythologist William Henry, is, "A place on Earth that is a shamanic trance portal to other worlds where energy pulsing (ringing) from our star, from other stars or star systems is easily received."

    Several pieces of architectural art align to the pyramids at Giza and the Sphinx in Egypt. Researcher Chad Stuemke states that the amphitheatre, fountain, and pyramid at Hart Plaza align precisely with the ancient Egyptian pyramids. Amphitheatres, Stuemke also notes, are instrumental to many stargate type parks as music is one of the highest forms of spiritual and mythological communications. And sounds, tunes or tones can trigger memories, activate emotions, and open our hearts, says William Henry.[281]

Did Woodward design his five-pentagram array of streets to imitate the Vitruvian Man of da Vinci? Did the energies of this possible sacrifice of four children eminent down into the temple? The largest Freemasonic center in the world, the Detroit Temple?

---

280 Dennis Cigler, Resume,
    http://www.petar.org/denniscigler/artist/exhibitions.html.
281 Stuemke, "Stargate."

The opera playing at the time of the killings at the Michigan Opera Theatre was *The Magic Flute,* by Mozart, an opera with starkly Freemasonic themes. Some contend that Mozart was killed after composing this piece for revealing Freemasonic Secrets. To round out the killing season the next year's opera was *Faust*, a story about a magician who makes a pact with the devil at the crossroads, exchanging his soul in the deal for unlimited power, knowledge and worldly pleasures.[282]

---

[282] Michigan Opera Theatre. Allesee Dance and Opera Resource Library Online Resources, Opera & Dance by Year, http://motlibrary.slis.wayne.edu/performance_search.html.

Chapter 14

A Web of Connections

Detective Rothstein wasn't your ordinary detective. He was appointed to work behind the scenes on the JFK assassination, and what happened with the Inslaw case and where it led, and what was really going on with all this sex trafficking in the United States. In short, he knew a lot of things about quite a few interconnected topics and the high-powered players who were in the know concerning these topics.

On one particular night working with the NYPD Rothstein had an informant in an apartment on E 64 Street in New York City. As Rothstein explained it, there were certain people in "our intelligence" community who were using this apartment to compromise some individuals and three little boys were murdered. He believes they were buried in Connecticut. They confronted the guy who they thought was responsible for the murders and authorities invoked "national security" and they were stopped. He said they had all the names, evidence and everything on it. Rothstein wondered just what part of the National Security Act allowed them to kill kids? He couldn't figure it out.[283]

---

[283] Mike Harris and James Rothstein. Mike Harris and James Rothstein - "Human Compromise," James Rothstein ex NYPD Detective Human Compromise Broadcast July 2013,
https://www.youtube.com/watch?v=exnrKpMgVwo.

The National Security Act was also evoked in the Franklin Scandal and this was duly noted by John DeCamp.

The National Security Act was implemented in 1947 after WWII. It reorganized the US Armed Forces and coordinated the US and British military and secret services so they could work together more efficiently. This was mapped out by Lord Maurice Hankey of Britain, whose organizational skills were second to none. According to Lord Vanstittart, Hankey had an incredible memory which grew into a repository of secrets.[284] The act was signed into law by President Truman and placed an extraordinary amount of emphasis on the coordination of national security with the intelligence community. The CIA was also created along with the position of the director of central intelligence, who was tasked with managing the CIA and overseeing the entire intelligence community. The basic stated goal of the National Security Act was "to provide a comprehensive program for the future security of the United States."[285]

How that goal fits in with the murdering of children is uncertain.

Apparently critical people are in strategic positions that can use "national security" as an excuse to commit crimes against the American people. As Detective Rothstein explained they had identified the person responsible for the murders of the three little

---

[284] Katharine Thomson, Archivist, "Maurice Hankey: Man of Secrets." *Churchill Archives Centre*, December 2016.
https://archives.chu.cam.ac.uk/collections/research-guides/hnky/.
[285] "National Security Council, United States agency," *Britannica*,
https://www.britannica.com/topic/National-Security-Council-United-States-agency.

boys in the apartment on E 64th Street and served him with a subpoena for the New York State Select Committee on Crime and the stipulation of national security was invoked so nothing could be done to prosecute this person. Essentially he was placed in the category of those "above the law."

Roy Cohn was one of those individuals who carefully maneuvered himself into a strategic position within the system in order to do dirty deeds for his client base. He had once explained to Detective Rothstein that he was there "to run the little boys." Cohn told him that if one of his people got caught it was his job to take care of it. And if they needed someone compromised? That was his job. Roy Cohn operated at the very highest levels of both government and business — and, Detective Rothstein added, another interesting place called the United Nations. Cohn also managed diplomatic dealings concerning the US, said Rothstein, and that, he said, was where the real power was.

"The three little boys were killed on E 64th Street and I always have believed those bodies were buried on Roy Cohn's farm in Greenwich, Connecticut."[286]

Roy Cohn was a lawyer and a dirty tricks political fixer. He was the attorney and personal confidant of Cardinal Spellman of New York, who was himself an FBI informant. He was President Trump's best friend and lawyer. His mentor, according to Trump. Cohn was infamous for throwing sex and drug parties at popular night spots such as Studio 54 and Le Club. Trump said he met Cohn at Le Club.[287]

---

286 Harris and Rothstein, "Compromise."
287 Barbara Boyd, "The British Empire Roots of American Social Control, Introduction: The Case of Donald Trump," *Executive Intelligence Review* 42, no. 32 (2015): 11-12.

Of course the depravity reached all the way to the top — to the White House. Henry Vinson, a DC madam, knew about all of this. He was introduced to some of the key players in this scene, Craig Spence and Lawrence King.

Vinson remarked that the suave Spence was the ultimate Prince of Darkness. He described him as extremely smart, manipulative, arrogant and who displayed a degree of narcissism that he had never encountered before.[288] Spence told Vinson that he blackmailed the rich and powerful and that his entire home was bugged for surveillance by the CIA with state-of-the-art equipment.[289] He nonchalantly told Vinson that he had taken an escort to the White House on a late-night tour. Vinson thought this was Spence's over the top bragging and completely unbelievable, so he checked it out with the escort in question. The escort then confirmed what Spence had said, that they had pulled up to the White House gate, and the Secret Service personnel had instantly waved him through the gate.[290]

Craig Spence's pal Lawrence King, of the Franklin Credit Union and sex trafficking ring scandal, divulged to Henry Vinson that he and Spence operated an interstate pedophile network that flew children from coast to coast. He also told him that they had a clientele of very powerful pedophiles who enjoyed and took pleasure in murdering children. Vinson was shocked at this

---

288 Henry W. Vinson with Nick Bryant, *Confessions of a D.C. Madam — The Politics of Sex, Lies, and Blackmail*, (Walterville, OR: Trine Day LLC, 2014), Loc 1148, Kindle Edition.
289 Vinson and Bryant, *Confessions*, Loc 1189.
290 Ibid.,Loc 1230.

disclosure and the fact that King seemed to be obsessed with the subject of murdering children.[291]

On May 3, 1994 the program *Conspiracy of Silence*, detailing the Franklin Cover-up and associated sex trafficking scandal, was scheduled to air on the Discovery Channel. Then certain influential members of congress applied pressure to the cable industry to not only stop the airing of the program, but to destroy all copies of the program. It had already been listed nation-wide in the US in the April 30-May 6 edition of *TV Guide* and newspaper supplements.

The program detailed how Lawrence King had cultivated contacts of the inner circle of Ronald Reagan's White House. He held extravagant parties for the influential and powerful and his lavish spending bought him a protected life. King was constantly lauded in the media. He then attracted the attention of the Internal Revenue Service.

In 1988 the FBI did an investigation which divulged that King had stolen 40 million dollars from the Franklin Credit Union. The allegations of sex trafficking and sexual abuse were well known and the FBI interviewed many victim's of Larry King's sex ring, but no action was taken regarding this area of the Franklin scandal.

So then in 1988 the state government of Nebraska decided to do a parallel investigation into King's criminality. A legislative committee was formed and the chairman was corn farmer and head of Nebraska's banking committee, state Senator Loran Schmit. Senator Schmit stated that they didn't want to collect innuendo but facts that could be proven in a court of law. The committee hired a

---

291 Ibid., Loc 1171.

special legal counsel and full-time professional investigators, Gary Caradori and Karen Ormiston. As the committee began their investigations, they found that the money trail led quickly to the original accusations of child abuse.

Investigators found new victims of King's pedophile network. Many were living on the streets of Omaha, Nebraska. Many named the same men as those involved in the Boystown cases three years earlier. To get hard evidence, the investigators recorded their new witnesses on videotape. Senator Schmit was shocked at the names that showed up on the list since he knew many of the individuals.

Schmit said that Boys Town came up in particular during the course of the investigation and it was very difficult to get information concerning this institution. He mentioned that he couldn't get any information when he visited there and neither could investigator Gary Caradori. Boys Town remained unwilling to discuss its involvement with Larry King; filmmakers were banned from filming at the institution and the public affairs director refused any interviews.

Investigator Karen Ormiston said it was Larry King who was at the center of transporting kids around the country. The airplanes were usually registered in his name, and leased in his name. They were also paid for by Larry King.[292]

Since Larry King flew coast to coast, it seems that he would have been aware of Francis Shelden's operation in Michigan and

---

292 Programmed To Kill/Satanic Cover-Up Part 368 (*Conspiracy of Silence 1993*), *LOLFIELDANDLOVE*,
https://odysee.com/@LOLFIELDANDLOVE:5/programmed-to-kill-satanic-cover-up-345:9.

Shelden would have been aware of King's. Shelden also had a plane which he used to fly to North Fox Island.

Interestingly, it was the grandfather of Jon Benet Ramsey, James Ramsey, who was the director of the Michigan Aeronautics Commission from 1957 to 1979 during the period that Francis Shelden had his airstrip constructed to fly children and pedophiles to his island.[293] The Michigan Aeronautics Commission (MAC) is responsible and empowered by state law to make rules and regulations governing all airports and aeronautical activities within the state of Michigan.[294] Strangely enough Ramsey had also lived in Nebraska, home of the Franklin scandal, and was director of the Nebraska Aeronautics Commission from 1947 to 1956.[295]

Nick Bryant, author of the *The Franklin Scandal: A Story of Powerbrokers, Child Abuse & Betrayal* talked about the number of parallels between the Epstein case and the Franklin scandal. He said that both flew children from coast to coast with impunity. And both cases had sources of wealth that were somewhat "ambiguous." Both cases were also covered up by law enforcement. In the case of Lawrence King, it was federal and state law enforcement, and in the case of Jeffrey Epstein it was also federal and state law

---

[293] *CAVDEF*, "North Fox Island pedophile ring — JonBenet Ramsey connection,"
https://www.cavdef.org/w/index.php?title=North_Fox_Island_pedophile_ring

[294] Michigan State Government Department of Transportation, Michigan Aeronautics Commission (MAC),
https://www.michigan.gov/mdot/about/commissions-councils-committees/michigan-aeronautics-commission.

[295] *CAVDEF*, "North Fox."

enforcement. He added there was also a tremendous amount of harassment to the victims.[296]

Nebraska State Senator Loren Schmit was very disappointed with law enforcement and the FBI and how they treated the victims. He said they turned them into the offenders, so to speak, and instead of taking the evidence that was delivered to them by the victims and interrogating the persons the victims identified, they seemed to bear down and try to get the victims to change their story.

During the height of the Franklin scandal in Nebraska, Troy Boner, victim of Larry King's sex trafficking ring was brought into questioning by the FBI. Troy said,

The FBI was like, no, these kinds of things just don't happen, in the first interview I went to, and they don't believe a fucking thing I'm saying. They were appalled, but I realized that look in their eye back then. That look was *fear*. I had witnessed firsthand, things that would destroy this city. It's not going to be believed, they said. It will *not* be believed, they said. You *will* be found guilty of perjury. I mean, they weren't telling me maybe. They were saying there's no way. You go on with this story and you're going to jail. I mean, that was said to me direct.[297]

In February of 2003 Troy Boner died in a Texas psychiatric hospital.[298] Mysterious circumstances surround his death.[299]

---

[296] Nick Bryant and Dr Lori Handrahan Interview by Eraldo and Daryn, *Unplugged*, August 3.
https://www.youtube.com/watch?v=_ib_eerfa74
[297] Programmed to Kill, *Conspiracy of Silence*.
[298] Nick Bryant, *The Franklin Scandal: A Story of Powerbrokers, Child Abuse & Betrayal*, (Waterville, OR: Trineday LLC, 2012), 495.
[299] Tim Tate, "Tim Tate on the making of the Franklin Scandal documentary Conspiracy of Silence," May 2, 2013, *The Reisman Institute*,

From the strange deaths to the bizarre excuses of law enforcement losing evidence or clearly acting to obstruct justice, the cover-up continues in the Oakland County Child Killer case and many others. These cases are only allowed the light of day if discussed and disguised under an officially approved narrative.

Like the emperor who wore no clothes, the lies need to be unmasked not only to maintain a healthy justice system, but for the ultimate future of a justice system at all. For this current system not only betrays its citizens in these types of cases, but maintains a cloak of secrecy beholden to those in power that maintain they can do whatever they want to those seeking justice.

It's time the victims get justice — for now, and for future generations.

---

https://www.thereismaninstitute.org/external-articles/2020/5/30/conspiracy-of-silence.

Illustrations

The four Oakland County Child Killer (OCCK) victims

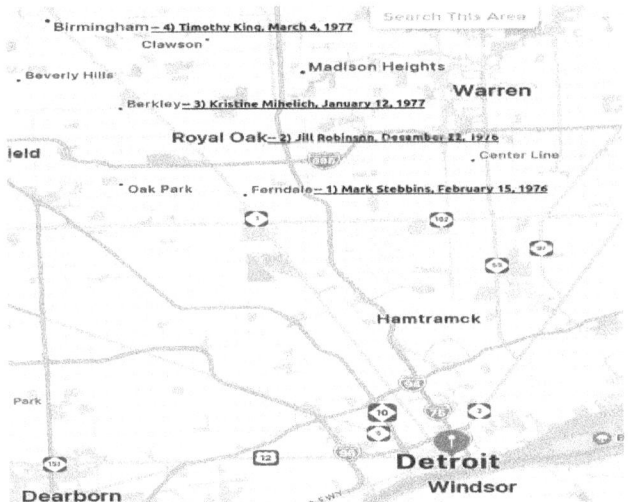

Victim's abduction location and timeline

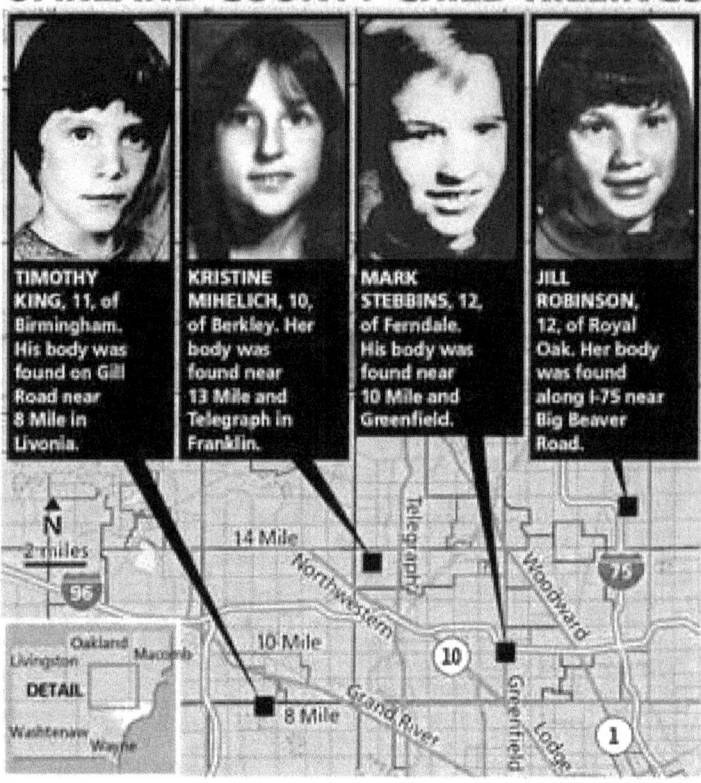

Suspect Christopher Busch

Drawing of what is thought to be of Mark Stebbins, found on Christopher Busch's bedroom wall.

John H. early 70s   Composite - Doug Wilson Hypnosis   John H. around 1975

Suspect John Hastings

Composite Drawings
June 9, 1977
Hypnosis of Witness Doug Wilson

Shelden left a trail of shock

By MARILYN WRIGHT
Record-Eagle staff writer

Copyright 1977, The Record-Eagle

TRAVERSE CITY — When Francis D. Shelden went into hiding to avoid prosecution on sexual misconduct charges he left behind a trail of shock, disbelief, anger, betrayal and, ultimately, suicide.

Although a year has passed since his disappearance, Shelden's name today remains on the lobby registry of the Buhl Building in Detroit.

And, authorities say, the 49-year-old Ann Arbor millionaire's business is being conducted by the fugitive's Birmingham attorney, L. Bennett Young.

A bachelor, licensed pilot, graduate geologist, part-time university professor, amateur botanist, land developer, oil consultant, market investor, reputed author, and sole owner of North Fox Island, Shelden's enterprises hop-scotch across the country: Oil leases in Kansas City, a ski lodge in Aspen, a land investment company in Denver, the Monroe Creek development in Charlevoix, and extensive stock holdings in a West Indies trust company.

Police records indicate Shelden cleaned out his Ann Arbor and North Fox Island residences shortly after Gerald S. Richards, an associate of Shelden's in Brother Paul's Childrens Mission, was arrested on criminal sexual conduct charges.

That was in July, 1976, approximately one week before state police obtained a search warrant for the Ann Arbor premises. A warrant was issued for his arrest on Dec. 7. A second warrant was issued a week later.

His prominent Grosse Pointe parents, the Alger Sheldens, say they have had

Part II

no contact with their son since he fled Michigan. Both are reported to be ill.

His brother, Alger Jr., is reported to have told authorities that he was hiring an armed guard and posting North Fox Island, the alleged site of illicit sexual conduct, to keep curiosity seekers and unauthorized police away.

Many residents of Charlevoix who knew Shelden as a gentlemanly scholar who was willing to share his good life, have yet to fully recover from the shock of his alleged sexual deviation and his disappearance.

Authorities, on the other hand, now believe that the purported benefactor had ulterior motives when he treated

youths to hunting trips on the island, skiing trips at Aspen, beach parties at the family estate on Antigua in the Caribbean, and set up trust funds for their college educations.

The tiny lakeside community was further jolted when shortly after Shelden disappeared, an 18-year-old youth whom the millionaire had befriended since he was nine, committed suicide.

Informed sources say Shelden wrote the youth from Miami, explaining that he would be "away for awhile" working on some "personal problems" but didn't want the youth to think he had forgotten about his promise to send him through college. A trust fund had been set up, Shelden wrote, to be administered by his brother, Alger Jr. A simple phone call would put the money in the youth's hands, Shelden said in the letter.

Three days after the warrant for Shelden's arrest was issued, and one day prior to the charges being publicly exposed in the Record-Eagle, the young man put a rifle in his mouth and pulled the trigger.

And, FBI agents say they plan to conduct a follow-up interview with another Charlevoix youth who was a frequent traveling companion of Shelden's. The young man was reported to be attending college on a similar trust fund.

Authorities say the young man recently has been driving Shelden's car which has been abandoned at the Charlevoix airport. Airport officials confirm that the car has been removed from the parking lot. They couldn't say who drove it away.

On the same day that the first young man's letter was sent from Miami, Oct. 13, 1976, another letter purportedly by Shelden was sent to Cranbrook Science Institute in Bloomfield Hills. That

Francis D. Shelden
...disappeared last year

letter, submitting his resignation as a member of the board of directors of the exclusive educational community, was postmarked from Kearney, N.J., where Adam Starchild, the Church of the New Revelation, and Ocean Living Institute are all located.

About that same time, Starchild was reportedly negotiating the sale of Shelden's plane through Combsgate Aviation in Denver, Colo.

In January of this year, Shelden resigned from the board of directors of Boys Republic, Inc., a Farmington Hills residential center for the treatment of emotionally disturbed young boys. The envelope, bearing the name and address of the family firm, Shelden Land Co., was postmarked Jan. 19, from Detroit.

That was the last public word from Francis D. Shelden.

. Next: A profile of another suspected child pornographer wanted by police.

JOHN McKINNEY, in a 1970 photo.

Mystery woman seen with John McKinney in a restaurant shortly before he was murdered.

Bibliography

Affidavit for Search Warrant. State of Michigan. Oakland County. Lieutenant Detective Patrick T. Sullivan. February 19, 1976.

Appleman, J. Reuben. *The Kill Jar: Obsession, Descent, and a Hunt for Detroit's Most Notorious Serial Killer.* New York: Simon and Schuster, 2018. Kindle Edition.

Aquino, Michael A. *The Church of Satan.* 5th ed. San Francisco, CA., 2002. https://ia802803.us.archive.org/9/items/michael-a-aquino-church-of-satan/michael-a-aquino-church-of-satan.pdf.

Berthiaume, Andy podcast. November 2018. "Alpena Witness." 1-6 segments. https://catherinebroad.blog/2020/09/22/alpena-witness/.

Birmingham Detective Bureau. Detectives Chambers and Solomon. Interview of Joy Colby. 4:10 pm, September 28, 1977.

Birmingham Detective Bureau. Detectives Chambers and Solomon. Interview of Marie Meredith. 1:30 pm, September 27, 1977.

Birmingham Police Department, check on artist of batik.

Birmingham Police Department. Detective Bureau. Detective Richard Chambers and Officer Larry Solomon. Homicide. 3:58 pm, September 21, 1977.

Birmingham Police Department. Detective Bureau. Homicide of John McKinney. Detective Richard Chambers. 3:07 pm, September 21, 1977.

Birmingham Police Department. Detective Bureau. Homicide of John McKinney. Interview of Steve Accomando. Det. Richard Chambers. 10:04 am, September 22, 1977.

Birmingham Police Department. Narrative Report. Detective Fraser. Crime Scene Homicide Investigation of John McKinney, September 20, 1977.

Birmingham Police Department. Narrative Report. Detectives Winkelmann and Marble. Psychic Helen Edwards. October 31, 1977.

Birmingham Police Department. Narrative Report. Follow-up Investigation. Sergeant Mohr. September 20, 1978.

Birmingham Police Department. Narrative Report. Follow-up Investigation. Sergeant Mohr. October 9, 1978.

Birmingham Police Department. Narrative Report. Follow-up Investigation. Sargeant Mohr. October 26, 1977.

Birmingham Police Department. Narrative Report. Homicide of John McKinney. Detectives Winkelman and Marble. September 22, 1977.

Birmingham Police Department. Narrative Report. Interview of Freda Riccardo. Detective Solomon. 3:45 pm, September 27, 1997.

Birmingham Police Department. Narrative Report. Interview of Martin Hoogasian. Sergeant Mohr. September 27, 1977.

Birmingham Police Department. Narrative Report. Interview of Peggy DeSalle. Detectives Marble and Solomon. October 11, 1977.

Birmingham Police Department. Narrative Report. Sergeant Mohr and Detective Solomon. September 26, 1977.

Birmingham Police Department. Narrative Report. Sergeant Mohr. September 27, 1977.

Birmingham Police Department. Narrative Report. Sergeant Mohr. October 19, 1977.

Birmingham Police Department. Narrative Report. Sergeant Mohr. October 28, 1977.

Birmingham Police Department. Narrative Report. Sergeant Malcolm Mohr. December 2, 1977.

Birmingham Police Department. Narrative Report. Sergeant Malcolm Mohr. December 12, 1977.

Birmingham Police Department. Narrative Report. To Department of Public Safety Intelligence Division. Phoenix, Arizona. Sergeant Malcolm Mohr. November 4, 1977.

Bosley, Walter and Richard B. Spence. *Empire of the Wheel: Espionage, Murder and the Occult in Southern California.* California: Corvos Books, 2011. Kindle Edition.

Boyd, Barbara. "The British Empire Roots of American Social Control, Introduction: The Case of Donald Trump." *Executive Intelligence Review* 42, no. 32 (2015): 11-12.

Britannica."National Security Council, United States agency." https://www.britannica.com/topic/National-Security-Council-United-States-agency.

Broad, Catherine. Comments. "McKinney." https://catherinebroad.blog/2015/04/20/mckinney/#comments.

Broad, Cathy. Comments. "Sloan's deviant days in Pennsylvania," https://catherinebroad.blog/2021/12/06/sloans-deviant-days-in-pennsylvania/.

Broad, Catherine. "From the FBI FOIA response re: documents relating to witness Doug Wilson's statements in the OCCK investigation," https://catherinebroad.blog/2013/05/24/from-the-fbi-foia-response-re-documents-relating-to-witness-doug-wilsons-statements-in-the-occk-investigation/.

Broad, Catherine. "Helen Dagner OCCK." *What the Hell is the Deal with the Oakland County Child Killer?* https://catherinebroad.blog.

Broad, Catherine. "Mark Douglas Stebbins," https://catherinebroad.blog/2024/02/15/mark-douglas-stebbins/.

Broad, Catherine. "Oakland County Child Killer Update Meeting, April 21, 2006, OCCK Tips Final." *What the Hell is the Deal with the Oakland County Child Killer?* https://catherinebroad.blog.

Broad, Catherine. "Shelden's Stain on all of Michigan and Beyond." https://catherinebroad.blog/2022/02/03/sheldens-stain-on-all-of-michigan-and-beyond/.

Broad, Catherine. "Thank you Doug Wilson," https://catherinebroad.blog/2013/02/04/thank-you-doug-wilson/.

Broad, Catherine. "Tullock-File-DPD-Infor-documents-Final-1." *What the Hell is the Deal with the Oakland County Child Killer Investigation?*, Special Assignment. Timothy King Homicide. March 30, 1977, 62. https://catherinebroad.blog/wp-content/uploads/2022/02/Tullok-File-DPD-Info-documents-Final-1.pdf

Broad, Catherine. What the Hell is the Deal with the Oakland County Child Killer Investigation? https://catherinebroad.blog/.

Broad, Catherine. "Who Looks Most Like John Wayne Gacy?," https://catherinebroad.blog/2020/08/29/who-looks-most-like-john-wayne-gacy/.

Bryant, Nick. *The Franklin Scandal: A Story of Powerbrokers, Child Abuse & Betrayal.* Waterville, OR: Trineday LLC, 2012.

Bryant, Nick and Dr Lori Handrahan. Interview by Eraldo and Daryn. Unplugged. August 3. https://www.youtube.com/watch?v=_ib_eerfa74.

Burdman, Mark. "Pedophiles arrested in Britain: 'More powerful than the Mafia.'" *Executive Intelligence Review* 16, no. 8 (1989): 42-3.

Burdman, Mark. "Satanists escalate war against Western civilization." *Executive Intelligence Review* 16, no. 1 (1989): 63-4.

Campbell, Alan, "Stories Spark Memories of Strange Encounters on North Fox Island," *Leelanau Enterprise.* April 3, 2014. Local News.

@CASSANDRACOGNO. "1981: NAMBLA's distinguished British Pedigree, Martin Swithinbank, & the NY Director of Sexual Abuse Prevention." *Bits of Books, Mainly Biographies.* https://bitsofbooksblog.wordpress.com/2015/02/12/1981-nambla-britishpedigree/.

Choucha, Nadia. *Surrealism and the Occult: Shamanism, Magic, Alchemy, and the Birth of an Artistic Movement.* Rochester, VT: Destiny Books, 1992.

Cigler, Dennis. Resume. http://www.petar.org/denniscigler/artist/exhibitions.html.

City of Birmingham Police Department. Detective Bureau. Detective Richard Chambers. Homicide. 3:17 pm, September 20, 1977.

City of Birmingham Police Department. Detective Bureau. Detective Richard Chambers and Officer Larry Solomon. Homicide. 3:58 pm, September 21, 1977.

City of Birmingham Police Department. Narrative Report: Follow-up Investigation. Homicide. Officer L. Solomon. 10:10 am, September 21, 1977.

City of Birmingham Police Department. Narrative Report. Homicide. Officer L. Solomon. 10:10 am, September 27, 1977.

City of Livonia. Narrative Report. "Oakland County Child Killings. Homicide of Timothy King. Busch and Greene Lead." D/Sgt. Cory Williams. Incident # 77-0006883. July 31, 2007.

The Collection. Senator Jack Faxon. Vimeo. Edited by Eric Johnston. Detroit, MI: Detroit Institute of Arts film. 2013. https://vimeo.com/78729226

Commonwealth of Pennsylvania vs Arch Sloan. Sodomy Section 501 and the Solicitation to Commit Sodomy 502. (Court of Common Pleas). Catherine Broad. https://catherinebroad.blog/2021/12/06/sloans-deviant-days-in-pennsylvania/.

Cribari, M.F. *Portraits in the Snow: The Oakland County Child Killings...Scandals and Small Conspiracies.* Denver, CO: Outskirts Press, Inc., 2011.

Danto, Bruce L., John Bruhns, Austin H. Kutscher and Lillian Kutscher, eds. *The Human Side of Homicide.* New York: Columbia University Press, 1982.

Danto, Bruce L. M.D., Letter to Birmingham Police Department. September 22, 1977.

Decades of Deceit: A True Story of the King Family Search for the Oakland County Child Killer. Unedited Comments, Dated April, May and July 2013. Prod. by RW Productions, LLC. https://rwpmi.com. Distributed by Tim King Fund, 2013; Birmingham, MI. DVD.

DeCamp, John W. *The Franklin Cover-Up: Child Abuse, Satanism, and Murder in Nebraska.* 2nd ed. Lincoln: AWT Inc., 1996.

Detective Cory Williams. Narrative Report. Livonia Police Department.

Detective Malcolm Mohr and Special Investigator for the Oakland Prosecutor's Office James O'Hearn. Narrative Report. Interviews of Douglas Wayne Webster and Lewis Davis. January 13, 1978.

Detectives Marble and Winkelman. Narrative Report. Information from Douglas Courtmer. September 23, 1977.

Detectives Solomon and Marble. Narrative Report, Interview of John Mark McKinney. September 27, 1977.

Detroit Police Department. Detectives Bone and Turney. Wayne Forest West Interview. 3:00 pm. April 18, 1977.

Doug Wilson Hypnosis Session with Dr Rossi. Narrative Report. Lieutenant Kalbfleisch.

EIR Investigative Team. "New evidence links CAN 'cult awareness; network to satanists," *Executive Intelligence Review* 18, no.32 (1991): 66-7.

Email message, Denise Powell (MSP) to Don Tullock (oakland.gov). *What the Hell is the Deal with the Oakland Child Killer?* Catherine Broad. https://catherinebroad.blog.

"Eye of the Chickenhawk." *The Hotstar.* https://thehotstar.net/eyeofthechickenhawk.html.

Federal Bureau of Investigation. Airtel Communication from Denver to Detroit. Frances Duffield Shelden — Fugitive, November 10, 1977. (Detroit, MI, 1977).

Firestone, Katherine Craker. *The Fox Islands North and South: Lake Michigan Islands.* Volume II. Northport: Michigan Islands Research., 1996.

FOIA Appeal. Catherine Broad. https://catherinebroad.blog/2021/05/26/foia-appeal/.

Georgia Open Records Request. Catherine Broad. https://catherinebroad.blog/2021/04/28/john-hastings-2/.

Gosch, Noreen N. *Why Johnny Can't Come Home*. West Des Moines: The Johnny Gosch Foundation, 2000.

Gunderson, Ted. Interview. "FBI's Lanning sides with Satan, says former top bureau official." *Executive Intelligence Review* 17, no. 23 (1990): 66-7.

Harris, Mike and James Rothstein. Human Compromise. James Rothstein ex NYPD Detective. Broadcast July 2013. https://www.youtube.com/watch?v-exmKpMgVwo.

Helen Dagner Notes. Catherine Broad. *What the Hell is the Deal with the Oakland County Child Killer?* https://catherinebroad.blog/.

HelenDagner. OCCK Archives. Part 16. https://www.youtube.com/watch?v=6wL6wnN_d_g.

Heri, Sesh. *The Handprint of Atlas.* Highland, CA: Corvos Books, 2010.

Information Statement. Sergeant Malcolm Mohr and Officer Larry Solomon. Interview of Mark McKinney, son of victim.

Information Statement. Sergeant Malcolm Mohr and Officer Larry Solomon. Interview of Michael Patten, CPA to victim. 2:40 pm. September 22, 1977.

Interview of Lester Arwin.

Interview: Mr Wayne West. Detectives Bone and Turney. Detroit Police Department. 3:00 pm, April 18, 1977.

Investigative Follow-up. Homicide. Mark Stebbins. Gerald Stonebraker. February 19, 1976.

Kaczynski, Richard. *Panic in Detroit.* New York: Sekhmet Books, 2015.

Kaushal, Ambrish. "Post Mortem Artefacts," Journal of Evolution of Medical and Dental Sciences. 8, no. 38 (2019): 1.

Keenan, Marnie Rich. *The Snow Killings: Inside the Oakland County Killer Investigation.* Jefferson, NC: Exposit. 2020.

LeBreton, Alexandre. *MKULTRA, Ritual Abuse and Mind Control: Tools of Domination for the Nameless Religion.* Dublin, Ireland: Omnia Veritas Limited, 2021.

Liebowitz, Ira. "The child pornography lobby protects cults, drugs, and mass murder," *Executive Intelligence Review* 10, no. 49 (1983): 27-9.

Mark, Joshua J. "Clergy, Priests & Priestesses in Ancient Egypt." March 7, 2017. *World History Encyclopedia*. https://www.worldhistory.org/article/1026/clergy-priests—priestesses-in-ancient-egypt/.

McChesney, Clifton. Michigan State University. Letter to Sargeant Mohr and/or Lieutenant Kalbfleisch. October 1, 1977.

McGowan, David. *Programmed to Kill: The Politics of Serial Murder.* Lincoln, NE: iUniverse, 2004.

McIntyre, Tommy. *Wolf in Sheep's Clothing: The Search for a Child Killer.* Detroit, MI: Wayne State University Press, 1988.

McKinney, John. Letter to Doug Webster. March 22, 1977.

Michigan Opera Theatre. Allesee Dance and Opera Resource Library. Online Resources. Opera & Dance by Year. http://motlibrary.slis.wayne.edu/performance_search.html

Narrative Report. Southfield Police Department. 11:50 am. February 19, 1976.

National Bank of Detroit v. Francis D. Shelden, 730 F.2d 421 (6th Cir. 1984).

Noble, William T. "Black Magic Once Detroit Cult Lives Ruined Decades Ago by Sorcerer Aleister Crowley." *The Detroit News.* January 26, 1958.

"North Fox Island pedophile ring — JonBenet Ramsey connection." *CAVDEF.* https://www.cavdef.org/w/index.php?title=North_Fox_Island_pedophile_ring

Oakland County Child Killer Investigation. Georgia Highway Patrol/Polygraph. Michigan Department of State Police. Supplemental Incident Report. October 9, 2009, https://catherinebroad.blog/2021/01/13/john-hastings/.

Oakland County Medical Examiner. "Mark Douglas Stebbins Autopsy, 1976." https://catherinebroad.blog/wp-content/uploads/2022/02/Stebbins-Autopsy-Final.pdf.

Oakland County Prosecutor's Office. Detective Jim A'Hearn. Telephone Interview. 2:30 pm. September, 29, 1977.

"Part 2: The Whole Story of the Spartacus International Gay Guide, by its founder John D. Stamford and how Bruno Gmünder made the bargain of his life." *BrunoLeaks*. https://brunoleaks.blogspot.com/2011/08/2teil-die-ganze-geschichte-vom.html.

Programmed To Kill/Satanic Cover-Up Part 368 (Conspiracy of Silence 1993), LOLFIELDANDLOVE, https://odysee.com/@LOLFIELDANDLOVE:5/programmed-to-kill-satanic-cover-up-345:9.

Royal Oak narrative report. Detectives Meitzner and Stinson. Jill Robinson Homicide, 76-26637. December 26, 1976.

Sergeant Mohr and Detective Winkelman. Narrative Report. Interview of Martin Hoogasian. September 19, 1977.

Sergeant Mohr. Narrative Report. September 27, 1977.

Sergeant Malcolm Mohr and Officer Larry Solomon. Interview of Cary Wilkie. 3:05 pm. September 22, 1977.

Sexual Exploitation of Children: Hearings Before the Subcommittee on Crime of the Committee on the Judiciary House of Representatives, Ninety-Fifth Congress, First Session on Sexual Exploitation of Children. May 23, 25, June 10 and September 20, 1977. (Serial No. 12) Statement of Gerald S. Richards. Jackson State Prison. Jackson, Mich.

"Slain Girl's Father is Angry at Police," *The Detroit News*. March 27, 1977.

Southfield Police Dept. Narrative Report. Detective Bureau Follow-Up, 2003.

Special Assignment. March 29, 1977 and April 6, 1977.

Special Assignment. Timothy King Homicide. March 30, 1977, 8:00 am to 10:00 pm.

Special Assignment. Timothy King Homicide. Notes.

Spence, Richard B. *Secret Agent 666: Aleister Crowley, British Intelligence and the Occult.* Port Townsend, WA: Feral House, 2008.

State of Michigan. Regional Crime Detection Laboratory. Laboratory Report. Homicide, John McKinney. Firearms. October 5, 1977.

Stuemke, Chad. "Stargate Detroit." *Chad Stuemke: Ancient Sacred Landscapes, Hidden Archeology and Modern Mystical Cities.* https://chadstuemke.com/stargate-detroit-i/.
Supplementary Report. Ferndale Police Department. Detective Frank. February 19, 1976, 12:40 pm.

Tape recorded conversation between Dr Sillery and Sergeant Malcolm Mohr.

Tape Recorded Interview of Edward Sloan. May 10, 2012.

Tate, Tim. "Tim Tate on the making of the Franklin Scandal documentary Conspiracy of Silence." May 2, 2013. *The Reisman Institute.* https://www.thereismaninstitute.org/external-articles/2020/5/30/conspiracy-of-silence.

Terry, Maury. *The Ultimate Evil.* NY: Barnes and Noble, 1987.

Thomson, Katharine. Archivist. "Maurice Hankey: Man of Secrets." *Churchill Archives Centre.* December 2016. https://archives.chu.cam.ac.uk/collections/research-guides/hnky/.

Tobias, Dr. Jerry. "Operation Burial Ritual." 1977. https://catherinebroad.blog/wp-content/uploads/2021/02/OCCK-Files-1.pdf

Tupman, Tracy W. "Theatre Magick: Aleister Crowley and the Rites of Eleusis." Ph.D dissertation. Ohio State University. 2003.

United States Department of Justice. Federal Bureau of Investigation. Francis Duffield Shelden, (Unlawful Flight to Avoid Criminal Prosecution — Sexual Criminal Conduct). Detroit, Michigan.

Videotaped Interview of Edward Sloan. May 17, 2012.

Vinson, Henry W. with Nick Bryant. *Confessions of a D.C. Madam — The Politics of Sex, Lies, and Blackmail.* Walterville, OR: Trine Day LLC, 2014.

W., Cory. Comments. "More," https://catherinebroad.blog/2023/08/27/more-5/.

Ward, Hiley. "One Grotto Becomes 'Occultic' Church: Satan Rift Centers in Detroit." *Detroit Free Press*. March 25, 1972.

Wayne County Prosecutor's Office Grand Jury investigation. The Homicide of Timothy King. Body found in Livonia in 1977. Reporting Officer: Detective Cory M. Williams (WCPO). October 2010.

Webster, Doug. Letter to John McKinney. April 12, 1977.

Webster, Nesta H. *Secret Societies and Subversive Movements*. London: Boswell Printing and Publishing Co., LTD., 1924.

Wheatley, Maria. *Divining Ancient Sites: Insights into their creation*. Marlborough: Celestial Songs Press, 2014.

Wikipedia. "Adam Starchild." https://en.wikipedia.org/wiki/Adam_Starchild.

Wikipedia. "M-1 (Michigan highway)." https://en.wikipedia.org/wiki/M-1_(Michigan_highway).

Wilson, Ellen. "OCCK is Huge." *Wilson's Words and Pictures*. https://wilsonswordsandpictures.com/occk-is-huge/.

Winfrey, Lee Winfrey. "Devil's Followers Increase." *Detroit Free Press*. April 13, 1971.

Wright, Marilyn. "Fugitive Warrants Requested." *Traverse City Record Eagle*, February 11, 1977.

Wright, Marilyn. "Shelden Left a Trail of Shock." *Traverse City Record Eagle,* Michigan, December 1977. newspaperarchive.com.

Wright, Marilyn. "Unrest Helped Unravel Nationwide Web." *Traverse City Record Eagle,* April 4, 1977.

www.ingramcontent.com/pod-product-compliance
Lightning Source LLC
Chambersburg PA
CBHW070759040426
42333CB00060B/1016